Issue 26, February 2026

AUSTRALIAN FOREIGN AFFAIRS

CONTRIBUTORS

SHIRO ARMSTRONG is professor of economics at the Australian National University.

LUKE BROWN is a climate strategy and public policy adviser and a former Australian diplomat.

MELISSA CONLEY TYLER is the executive director of the Asia-Pacific Development, Diplomacy & Defence Dialogue (AP4D).

RICHARD HOLDEN is Scientia professor of economics at UNSW Business School.

ROBERT LAW is a board member of the Australia-Indonesia Institute.

ANTHONY MILNER is emeritus professor of Asian history at the Australian National University.

DAVID UREN is a senior fellow at the Australian Strategic Policy Institute and a former economics editor of *The Australian*.

Australian Foreign Affairs is published three times a year by Australian Foreign Affairs Pty Ltd. Publisher: Morry Schwartz. Editor-in-chief: Erik Jensen. ISBN 9781760646196. ISSN 2208-5912. Subscriptions: 1-year print and digital subscription (3 issues): $79.00 within Australia incl. GST. 1-year digital-only auto-renew: $49.00. Payment may be made by MasterCard, Visa or Amex, or by cheque made out to Schwartz Books Pty Ltd. Payment includes postage and handling. Subscribe online at www.australianforeignaffairs.com, email subscribe@australianforeignaffairs.com or phone 1800 077 514 / 61 3 9486 0288. Correspondence should be addressed to: The Editor, Australian Foreign Affairs, 22–24 Northumberland Street, Collingwood, VIC, 3066 Australia Phone: 61 3 9486 0288 / Fax: 61 3 9486 0244 Email: enquiries@australianforeignaffairs.com. Editor: Jonathan Pearlman. Deputy Editor: Julian Welch. Associate Editor: Chris Feik. Design: L.B. Stephens. Production Coordination: Marilyn de Castro. Typesetting: Tristan Main. Cover image: Suriyapong Thongsawang. Printed in Australia by McPherson's Printing Group.

EDITOR'S NOTE
Who Won?

JONATHAN
PEARLMAN

In April 2025, Donald Trump unveiled his long-promised tariffs for more than 180 countries, leaving the United States with its highest level of tariffs since before the Great Depression.

But Trump's so-called "reciprocal" tariffs did not – as he claimed – match other countries' tariffs. Instead, the rates were based on the trade deficit that each country had with the United States. James Surowiecki, a commentator who was among the first to identify how the new rates had been calculated, described them as "just made-up numbers". "What extraordinary nonsense this is," he observed.

The reciprocal tariffs, along with the other wildly fluctuating tariffs and barriers that Trump has imposed in his second term, have left foreign leaders with the delicate task of rejecting them without risking retribution from the notoriously vindictive US president.

Australia, for instance, was presented with a "reciprocal" rate of 10 per cent even though the United States has a trade surplus with it, which – according to the White House's calculation method – should have made the tariff a negative number. Wisely, Australian prime minister Anthony Albanese responded by sticking to the facts, which amounted to a potent attack. A reciprocal tariff, he pointed out, "would be zero" for Australia. "The administration's tariffs on Australia have no basis in logic," he concluded.

But Trump's tariffs have not merely wrought economic damage and recast Washington's foreign relationships; they have also served as a crude marker of the ways in which the global order has been changing. Over the past decade, the United States, the world's largest economy, has abandoned its decades-long project of championing global trade. The push for free trade had been bipartisan – as was its abandonment.

For the Democrats, this reversal was highlighted by the decision of Hillary Clinton, as a presidential candidate in October 2015, to oppose the ten-nation Trans-Pacific Partnership (TPP) trade deal. Just three years earlier, Clinton, visiting Australia as secretary of state, had described the deal as "the gold standard in trade agreements" and a pathway to "open, free, transparent, fair trade". But, facing Bernie Sanders in the primaries, she followed his lead and opposed the deal.

For the Republicans, the reversal can be seen through the trajectory of Marco Rubio, who, competing in the Republican primaries in 2015, said support for the TPP was a pillar of his foreign policy. The deal, he wrote in *The Wall Street Journal,* will "further our strategic goals in Asia and ... unleash free-market forces in the world's most dynamic region". Today, Rubio, who is secretary of state, opposes the TPP and backs Trump's tariffs. "We need to get back to a time where we are a country that can make things, and to do that, we have to reset the global order of trade," he told reporters after Trump announced his reciprocal tariffs.

And so the world's two economic powerhouses are the United States, which is reverting to protectionism, and China, which practises an opaque and at times punitive version of state capitalism.

Australia remains committed to the open global trading order that has underpinned its prosperity. But the simple logic of this system, and of its opportunities and benefits, is losing its force in an age of quick-fix huckster politics and deepening inequalities. Australia can and should press the case for open trade, but it must also examine the mechanics of the new economic order that is emerging and consider its best options for preserving growth without abandoning principles or logic.

WEAPONS OF CHOICE

Australia and the new economic order

SHIRO ARMSTRONG

Australia's national security rests on two crucial pillars: the US alliance and the multilateral trading system. These two pillars have anchored Australia's security since the 1942 wartime pacts with the United States, which laid the basis for the creation of the rules-based economic order at Bretton Woods.

The trading system that grew out of the General Agreement on Tariffs and Trade (GATT), later the World Trade Organization (WTO), has protected the global economy from a repeat of the problems of the 1930s: stagnation aggravated by closed markets, the deployment of economic weaponry for political coercion, and economic rivalry feeding political conflict. Those who were negotiating the Bretton Woods institutions were not blind to security threats: war was still raging. Indeed, they designed a system that would as far as possible disentangle security tensions from economic interactions, so that the self-reinforcing spiral of rearmament and protectionism, which provided the spark for the inferno of World War II, could be avoided.

The Bretton Woods architecture was never perfect and has gone through many changes. But it has for the past eight decades kept the global economy open, given countries confidence to deepen their engagement in trade and fostered unprecedented development, prosperity and security.

The trading system, with the GATT/WTO at its core, has helped sustain a cooperative outcome whereby all countries that signed onto it were better off. It has acted as a brake against protectionism, even in its current weakened state.

The arrangements prevented the unchecked use of raw political power to dominate trade outcomes. Governments could reap the benefits of trade by signing up to agreed multilateral rules, instead of relying on bilateral deals that exposed them to the pressures of power-based bargaining.

Countries with unresolved historical tensions, rivalries, mistrust and territorial disputes could open themselves up to trade and deepen economic interdependence. Nowhere is that more evident than in North-East Asia between China, Japan and

South Korea. The economic ties created a floor in the management of their political relations.

This system has been a source of resilience from shocks such as the Asian financial crisis and the global financial crisis (GFC). An open global economy offers a wide range of alternative suppliers and buyers, as was evident when Australian exporters were hit by Chinese trade sanctions in 2020. The WTO and its dispute settlement workaround, the Multi-Party Interim Appeal Arbitration Arrangement (MPIA), provided the off-ramp to that episode of trade coercion.

The system now faces the biggest test since its creation. The multilateral rules are outdated, and the United States, which led their creation and enforcement, has now turned spoiler. The rules have not been enforceable for much of the world since the US veto of the appointment of judges to the WTO's dispute settlement body. A total breakdown of the system would mean economic devastation and insecurity for Australia and its neighbours.

The risks of a world trade war are real and active

Contrary to a common view, the WTO is far from dead. Whether it survives the wholesale attack on trade rules and norms from Trump 2.0 will depend on how the rest of the world responds.

Trump's 2 April so-called Liberation Day "reciprocal tariffs" were higher than the US Smoot–Hawley tariffs that followed the stock market crash of 1929. What made the Smoot–Hawley tariffs so damaging, prolonging the 1930s depression, was the retaliatory spiral and contagion they caused. Trump's tariffs have not remained as high as his Liberation Day announcements and most of the world held the line on retaliation, but the US trade war on the world is by no means over.

Global markets have calmed from the gyrations around Trump's on-again, off-again tariff uncertainty. This respite is akin to the "Phoney War" before World War II – the eight months after the

Allies declared war on Germany but when little happened before the conflagration of World War II began. The global economy is potentially on a trajectory towards a 1930s world of strategic competition and closing markets. The risks of a world trade war are real and active. High-energy, careful diplomacy will be needed to avoid it.

UNITED STATES IN RETREAT

The unprecedented growth in prosperity and stability for an increasing proportion of humankind in the past eight decades would not have been possible without US leadership in underpinning the open global system.

The GFC of 2008 marked the beginning of a retreat from that leadership. Trump's Liberation Day tariff hit was a declaration of war against the rules-based order. This turn towards protectionism in the United States has been prompted by stagnant living standards, a maldistribution of the gains from progress – both trade and technological – and the lack of an effective social safety net, including universal healthcare. President Joe Biden's decision to preserve Trump's protectionist policies from his first term confirms that Trump is a symptom rather than the cause of the problems America faces.

Prior to Trump's election in 2016, the average applied US tariff rate was 1 per cent. That rose to 2.9 per cent by the eve of Biden's presidency, mostly due to Trump 1.0's trade war with China. It rose to an average of 27 per cent after Liberation Day with tariffs on Chinese imports reaching 245 per cent, and 50 per cent for India, Brazil and others, imposed for a variety of seemingly random reasons. Countries have gone to war over much lower tariffs. Temporary truces have been reached with many countries, but the threat of tariffs is a daily reality under Trump 2.0.

The deals that countries are making with Trump to reduce tariffs – in most cases settling for rates that are higher than anything the United States has levied in the post-war period – directly undermine the most-favoured-nation treatment that is the basis for the rules-based order.

Tariffs overwhelmingly hurt the country that imposes them, and US consumers and businesses are beginning to pay the price. A sudden recognition of national self-interest and reversal of policy in Washington is unlikely anytime soon. In Trump's power-based world, US tariffs are sticky and here to stay. The motivations for them are deep and structural: many communities are worse off than they were a generation ago, even as the US economy has grown strongly and the richest Americans have become much richer. There is no quick domestic or international fix. Any future president who tries to reduce or remove tariffs will likely have to extract concessions from other countries.

For Trump, trade is a zero-sum fight. He rejects the principle of mutual benefit and sees the United States as needing to win in some way in every trade exchange.

Washington now resents its own exorbitant privilege of being able to borrow more cheaply than other countries and run persistent trade and current-account deficits without facing the usual market penalties because of the acceptance of the US dollar as the world's currency. The United States is seeking to dismantle the existing order, effectively exporting its domestic governance disorder of "might is right" to the rest of the world.

Trade deficits, which Trump treats as a fundamental evil, are simply the accounting counterpart of foreigners' longstanding confidence in the United States as a destination for investment. The flip side of a current-account deficit is a capital-account surplus: the US trade deficit is driven by its domestic savings and investment imbalance, including its huge budget deficits. If Trump succeeds in reducing the US trade deficit, it will only be because he has convinced the rest of the world that the US policy environment has become too risky for locating long-term investment in America.

Trump's belief that trade deficits are a transfer of wealth is the main justification for his tariffs. Others in his administration want autarky, onshoring, a rewriting of the Bretton Woods system and primacy over China, but Trump has at least been consistent since the

1980s in his misguided reasons for favouring tariffs. His zero-sum thinking, where only one side wins, is causing negative-sum outcomes, where everyone loses, and the United States will eventually lose most. Opening up to trade is mutually beneficial, but the opposite is also true: closing down trade is mutually harmful.

The United States has been the biggest beneficiary of the system that it now threatens to tear down and has articulated no clear alternative. The rest of the world must protect the system from contagious disorder and keep it open for the United States to rejoin when it is ready. A multilateral trading system absent the most powerful country in the world will be difficult to sustain but is the best option for now.

The United States accounts for only 15 per cent of world trade so it is up to those nations holding the remaining 85 per cent, many of which will be resistant to US coercive power, to protect the scaffolding of the multilateral system. The signs since Liberation Day are that the rest of the world wants to keep trading, with trade growing fastest in the developing world.

Many, of course, blame China for the current state of affairs. In the United States there is regret about letting China into the WTO, because its political system is supposedly incompatible with the rules-based system, resulting, the argument suggests, in the "China shock" of job losses and US deindustrialisation. This logic rewrites history to claim China was supposed to become more like "us" if let into the WTO. The reality is the WTO and other multilateral institutions include countries with varying degrees of political liberalisation. What matters is their adherence to the rules, and by that count China's track record, while far from perfect, is better than that of the United States and the European Union. China's and the other powers' adherence to WTO trade rules is there for all to see on the WTO website.

The outdated rules in the WTO do not take account of state subsidies, for example, that tilt the playing field in favour of China. The WTO has been impotent when it comes to constraining subsidies generally, whether in agriculture or in the new wave of industry policies in developed and developing countries alike. New restraints on subsidies are being negotiated in regional agreements like the Comprehensive and Progressive Agreement for Trans-Pacific Partnership (CPTPP). China's bid to join the CPTPP would require it to fundamentally reform its state-owned sector and level the playing field.

The China shock argument – the idea that surges of cheap Chinese imports into the United States wiped out jobs and created the US rust belt – fails to recognise that much of the rest of the world that also experienced surges of Chinese imports did not suffer in the same way. Countries in South-East Asia that compete more closely with what China produces, as well as other manufacturers such as Japan and South Korea, managed the adjustment costs of shifting to new industries and shared the gains across society because of their better social protection systems.

China's economic reforms, especially those on the way to WTO accession, transformed it into a substantial market-based economy whose exports are dominated by private enterprises, including the presence of foreign-invested firms that account for around 40 per cent of China's exports. The adjustments in the global system to China's rise have not been easy. China has made the adjustment for other countries harder through widespread state intervention in strategic industries and its practice of economic coercion, which undermines trust in its reliability as a trading partner. But blaming China for the problems in the United States or in the WTO are misguided. Such arguments fail to consider the stake that China has in the established system, or the counterfactual world in which China, with its population of 1.3 billion people, were entirely outside of established rules.

KEEPING CHINA IN THE SYSTEM

The days are long gone when China could only accept the rules devised by others; it now has the economic weight to help make them. The economic and geopolitical adjustment to China's rise is certainly complicated by its less transparent system of government. The best, and perhaps only, way to manage that rise is within the established multilateral system to which China has signed up and in which it has a stake.

As the world's largest trading nation and a nation without any major formal allies, China is deeply dependent on the system that helps to manage its trade interests and exposure to economic coercion. Australia's and other countries' economic and political security in turn lie in sustaining China's dependence on that system and its multilateralist posture.

China has a demonstrated preference for enforceable trade rules, including through its membership of the MPIA. The MPIA duplicates the WTO's dispute settlement Appellate Body, enabling its fifty-seven member countries to resolve trade disputes peacefully among themselves. The United States has made it clear it will no longer be held to account by world trade rules.

A loss of confidence in the system by China would help unravel its trade with the rest of the world, destroying trade's pacifying effects. A Chinese economy and society that is less integrated in the global economy would bring more international political risks, not fewer. Interdependence acts as a constraint on China that does not eliminate the prospect of war but makes war more difficult and costly. That constraint is much stronger for an economy like China's than one like Russia's, which is not deeply integrated into regional or global trade and production networks.

With the United States vacating the field, many fear that China will grasp the mantle of leader of the multilateral system. But China's size does not substitute for the trust, moral authority or confidence from others that it has squandered. The smartest strategy is to press China to demonstrate its multilateral credentials through actions, not just words, instead of snuffing out its space on the multilateral stage. For example, there is concern among Australian and Japanese trade officials that a leaders' meeting led by the Association of

Southeast Asian Nations (ASEAN) to boost the Regional Comprehensive Economic Partnership (RCEP) agreement gives China too much of a platform as the United States retreats. But the leaders' meeting helps shape Chinese behaviour collectively: leaders, including from China, agreed in 2025 to deregulate their economies and rebalance growth – not-so-subtle code for increasing consumption in China to help ease pressures on other markets from the flood of Chinese exports.

There are concerns in Europe and elsewhere that China's mercantilist policies will leave many unable to compete with its manufacturing, and that there will be nothing to sell to China or compete on international markets with. But countries will always have a comparative advantage and China cannot make everything. The lessons from the shock in the United States from China's entry into the WTO are just as relevant for the shock that Europe fears: look to Asia, which managed to stay competitive and deepened integration in supply chains.

Some in Beijing (and in Washington) may think that China's large share of global trade can be wielded as a political tool, but the market forces that now entwine the Chinese economy and are the source of its modern success also constrain its international behaviour.

Chinese economic coercion – child's play compared to the economic coercion that Washington has now wreaked upon the world but tinged with its own brand of vindictiveness – has backfired economically or politically or both. The open global economy enabled alternative buyers and suppliers and protected countries that were targeted, with varying but limited cost.

To protect against Chinese coercion and a weakening rules-based system, Australia, Japan and Europe have begun deploying defensive economic measures. But restricting trade, investment and interdependence with China in the name of security risks a costly spiral. Using defensive measures to guard against limp coercion ultimately weakens the very trading system that provides the strongest protection from such coercion.

THE PROBLEM WITH SECOND-BEST STRATEGIES

Defensive, "second-best" strategies such as friendshoring, reshoring, diversification and protective industrial policy, while rational in isolation, erode the multilateral framework whose weakening they are meant to hedge against. And they make the return to a rules-based order more elusive.

As trust in shared rules erodes, policies that restrict commerce to insure against global risk are further fragmenting trade and investment flows. Rules-based trade *is* economic security.

Diversifying trade, much as investors might diversify their investments, might sound sensible but it is the opposite of trading according to comparative advantage, which is about specialising in what you're good at and selling to those willing to pay the highest price. Even for investors, "diversification is protection against ignorance", as Warren Buffett explains. "It makes little sense if you know what you are doing."

Australia can diversify its trade away from what market forces dictate but the more it succeeds in doing so, the poorer Australians will be. Forcing businesses to sell to smaller markets for less, based on security or vague policy rationales, threatens their viability.

"Friendshoring" – relocating supply chains, trade and investment towards trusted partners – makes the world only slightly bigger than "reshoring" or "onshoring", which bring manufacturing home, even if "friends" could easily be defined. Cutting out non-friends from supply chains concentrates risk, increases costs, reduces choices and leaves fewer buyers and

Restricting trade, investment and interdependence with China in the name of security risks a costly spiral

suppliers. Freezing countries out of markets because they have a different political system or are currently perceived as rivals turns them into permanent adversaries.

Treating all trading nations equally is fundamental to post-war rules-based trade. The level playing field is preserved through the principle of most-favoured-nation treatment, which rules out discrimination between trading partners. Its erosion moves the world towards "might is right" and has immediate implications.

The costs of decarbonisation, for example, are already high but will be much higher if supply chains are driven by geopolitics instead of market forces. Some may see China's overcapacity in the production of batteries, solar and electric vehicles as a threat but the global economy is not manufacturing enough of those goods and technologies. China, for the moment, seems willing to subsidise the global transition to net zero. It takes real economic illiteracy to shut them out of our markets.

The question with which policymakers must grapple is what is needed to once again create confidence in concentrated markets. In extremis, how can countries work with and around China to make critical minerals no longer critical – to build confidence that their purchases of Chinese minerals and goods or their exports to China will not be restricted when there are disagreements?

AUSTRALIA'S SLIDE INTO INSULARITY

As the weaponisation of trade becomes more threatening, Australia must aim to maintain openness and protect the multilateral trading system. Building confidence in open trade is crucial, particularly as uncertainty increases and the external environment becomes more hostile.

International trade is not about what is negotiated in trade agreements or even what happens in Geneva at the WTO. Those things matter, of course, but what ultimately matters is how external arrangements such as trade agreements are used to lock in that openness at home and to shape the international environment by negotiating new rules and keeping other markets open.

Nothing that President Trump or President Xi have done changes the cost–benefit calculus of economic openness. Barriers to trade and investment still harm the country imposing them the most. On this count, Australia could be doing better. Drift and slippage into economic insularity is leading to falling productivity and threatening the country's living standards.

Australia has unilaterally removed a suite of "nuisance" tariffs – low tariffs that cost more in compliance than they raise in revenue – in what has been the most significant trade reform in recent times. Two tranches of 500 nuisance tariffs in 2024 and 2025 were cut on goods such as toothbrushes, washing machines, fridges, tampons and tyres. But the effects of such measures are limited by over-regulation of importers. Australia is now one of the biggest users of anti-dumping measures to protect its domestic industries from what it considers unfairly priced imports, disproportionately targeting goods from China such as steel. Some of that is starting to look like the old made-to-measure protection, with anti-dumping tariffs on railway wheels that protect a local monopoly, for example. Australian businesses will not be globally competitive if they are shielded from competition in this way.

Australia also has the most restrictive foreign investment regime among all industrial countries, as measured by the Organisation for Economic Co-operation and Development. Chinese investment in Australia has shrunk, while it has grown in other countries. There are some legitimate areas for restriction of investment on security grounds, such as in defence-related industries or near defence sites, but they are limited. Former US national security adviser Jake Sullivan popularised the term "small yard, high fence" to describe protecting a narrow set of critical technologies and research (the small yard) behind stringent export and investment restrictions (the high fence), while allowing wider trade and investment flows to continue unimpeded. Australia's investment regime looks like a big yard surrounded by a high fence towards Chinese investment, leaving investors from all countries less confident about investment in Australia. If Australia abandons openness, the productive capacity of the economy will be reduced. For recent proof, look no further than the post-Brexit UK economy, where the decision to leave the European Union cost the British economy cumulative growth of between 6 per cent and 8 per cent.

Lessons from Trump's America and Brexit – about the maldistribution of economic gains and the need for social protections – must be taken seriously. The free trade consensus in Australia still appears intact, with the 2024 Lowy Institute Poll showing strong and rising support for free trade: 80 per cent of Australians say that open trade improves their standard of living, 77 per cent believe it benefits the economy and 71 per cent say it creates jobs. But the cost-of-living crisis, anaemic productivity growth and stagnant living standards are already causing anti-immigration sentiment in the community and are a recipe for a backlash against free trade.

Reforms that promote productivity and openness – such as welcoming more investment for decarbonisation – enable economies like Australia to remain close to the global technological frontier, a frontier increasingly defined by China. Coupled with Australia's social protections, they are a formula for preventing the growth of anti-globalisation sentiment.

Australia is a small open economy and a price taker – rather than a price setter – in the global market. As a middle power, it cannot alter the status quo unilaterally – that's what great powers are able to do – but it can lead coalitions to help shape its external environment. On that, Australia's track record is good. It was a leader in the creation of the Asia-Pacific Economic Cooperation (APEC) and the Cairns Group coalition of twenty countries that achieved liberalisation of agricultural trade within the WTO, and has been an active shaper of regional and global economic arrangements.

Australia's influence in Asia relies on credible commitments and trust, which some economic security policies risk eroding. This influence has come not from the backing of US power as its security ally, but from being an honest broker in a diverse region with countries of all shapes, sizes, systems and colours. Australia is most influential when it leads with ideas and diplomacy and treats all partners equally, not when it plays deputy sheriff in South-East Asia and the Pacific.

HOW TO FIX THE SYSTEM

Asia is Australia's primary theatre of policy initiative and action. The East Asian region accounts for 67 per cent of Australia's foreign trade. Australia is still in the most economically dynamic part of the world: Asia accounts for 60 per cent of global growth.

A strategy that treats South-East Asia as a global partner in defence of the multilateral trading system does not come naturally to a country psychologically used to engaging in Asia with the confidence of close political and cultural links to the North Atlantic backed by US power. But a strategy that forges a partnership with South-East Asia and East Asia may now be Australia's best chance of preserving the rules-based system on which its economic prosperity depends.

Australia's clearest path to protecting open trade is to work with the institution that is central to regional affairs: ASEAN. Since it was founded in 1967, ASEAN has delivered political stability to the diverse states of South-East Asia through its consensus-based decision-making and its emphasis on non-interference in internal affairs. These features appear to make ASEAN difficult to influence and often toothless. But when the stakes are high, ASEAN has time and again demonstrated its capacity for proactive responses.

ASEAN collectively held the line against Liberation Day tariffs even as Canada, China, the European Union and others threatened retaliation, risking contagion. ASEAN leaders doubled down on rules, openness and cooperation even as their economies were being flooded by cheap Chinese imports shut out of the US market. Some, like Indonesia's President Prabowo Subianto, announced a deregulation agenda to further open up, bringing some certainty to

Indonesian businesses and others in South-East Asia in the wake of these disruptions.

In response to Trump's tariffs and strategic competition between China and the United States, ASEAN launched a Geoeconomic Taskforce to consider geopolitics when making economic decisions and vice versa. It also convened a meeting of economic ministers and foreign ministers, the first time they have met together. ASEAN also elevated the RCEP process to a leaders' meeting for the first time since the agreement came into force.

It was ASEAN that launched the RCEP agreement in 2013 in response to rising protectionism and a Trans-Pacific Partnership (TPP) that threatened to divide ASEAN interests. RCEP is ASEAN-led, not China-led, and the world's biggest regional trade agreement in terms of GDP, trade and population. Indonesia navigated the conclusion of the deal in the face of rising protectionism, a pandemic and the US–China trade war. China is the biggest economy in that grouping – which also includes Australia, New Zealand, Japan and South Korea – but its influence is qualified by the ASEAN member states being in the driving seat. RCEP is ASEAN's strategy to help its members manage their China relationship to avoid being picked off bilaterally. Australia, Japan, New Zealand and South Korea have an interest in doubling down on ASEAN's strategy of enmeshing Chinese interests in an outwardly oriented RCEP.

Outside Trump's America, much of the world is keen on free trade and agreements continue to proliferate

Regional arrangements will be the frontline of defence of the multilateral trading system. The MPIA shows a WTO-minus-US world might be workable for now. Almost a third of the WTO's membership (comprising 34 per cent of global trade) have signed up to the MPIA to make the multilateral rules enforceable.

The other major regional agreement of consequence is the CPTPP, which was salvaged after the United States withdrew from the TPP. A key test for whether the RCEP and the CPTPP will be globally consequential is how open they are to new members. So far the United Kingdom has acceded to the CPTPP, while the RCEP is considering potential members such as Sri Lanka, Bangladesh and Hong Kong. But the real test for the CPTPP is how it handles China's and, to a lesser extent, Taiwan's bids to join. For now it is working on Costa Rican and Uruguayan accession, leaving China and Indonesia waiting in the queue.

Outside Trump's America, much of the world is keen on free trade and agreements continue to proliferate. The big free trade pacts are attracting more interest from countries wanting to join.

The promise of CPTPP entry is a powerful incentive for reform in China and Indonesia. Creating a process that allows China and Indonesia to demonstrate reform and that tests trust in their credentials on a path towards membership has the potential to transform Chinese state-owned enterprises and abolish export restrictions in Indonesia, for example. If they fail to reform, they should not be admitted, but a genuine process needs to start with the understanding that they will be admitted if they do.

A price for China's entry into the CPTPP could be a commitment to maintain the security of supply of critical minerals. For those in the MPIA, the RCEP and the CPTPP, there can be a mutual disarmament of economic weaponry.

It's through these regional arrangements and initiatives that Australia can best fix global problems. Making progress on a subsidy code – agreeing to what subsidies are reasonable and what are simply protectionist – and codifying exceptions for security, for example, is likely to be easier to do regionally than in the WTO. Those efforts could start in Asia, with ASEAN, China and Japan, and lead to arrangements that connect to Europe, Canada and other willing partners.

We do not need another world war to transition to a new global order. Saving the existing trading system is the priority, not throwing it away because of the challenges posed by the rise of China and the retreat of the United States. The post-war economic order has evolved and managed the rise of Japan and Asia. It can evolve again. Based on the principles of equal treatment and a level playing field, the aim is to achieve a rules-based, not a power-based, order.

Australia's weapon of choice in the world trade wars must be openness

Separate, overlapping regional trade agreements can only hold the multilateral system together if there is a reference point, such as the WTO, at its core and if the agreements are inclusive of aspirant members, not exclusive blocs based on geopolitics.

Free trade is not dead. The best response to rising protectionism and global uncertainty is strengthening free trade institutions rather than adopting defensive measures that weaken them. Australia's weapon of choice in the world trade wars must be openness, including a proactive effort at coalition-building to defend the global multilateral system, starting in its own backyard in Asia. ■

FOLLOW THE MONEY

Australia stuck in China's orbit

DAVID UREN

It was an unfortunate coincidence: Prime Minister Anthony Albanese embarked on his six-day tour of China in July 2025 on the same day the *Financial Times* reported that the Pentagon wanted to know what role its Australian and Japanese allies would play in the event of a military conflict over Taiwan. US Undersecretary of Defense for Policy Elbridge Colby, who had made the Pentagon's demands, followed the *FT* story, posting on social media: "Some among our allies might not welcome frank conversations." The United States itself has not declared what it would do if China's armed forces attacked Taiwan, and Albanese was not prepared to entertain hypotheticals about a war with his Chinese hosts as he was peppered with questions from the media scrum that accompanied his trip.

The awkward timing underlined the tension in Australia's great foreign policy fudge: that we can enjoy both the fruit of our economic relationship with China and the security afforded by our alliance with the United States.

Australia's security concerns about the threat posed by China had contributed to the severing of political relations between the two countries from 2020 to 2022 and the imposition of the most comprehensive set of trade bans China had ever imposed on any country.

Albanese said his trip was about stabilising the relationship. "It was at a bad point prior to our election in 2022," he noted. "Since then, we have seen over $20 billion of trade impediments removed and we're now exporting large amounts, in some cases more than we were before." He travelled with the chief executives of the four principal iron ore miners – BHP, Rio Tinto, Fortescue and Hancock Prospecting – as well as a bevy of other chief executives.

The Chinese authorities seemed satisfied with the Labor government's decision to stop open criticism of China (which Albanese has described as "putting away the loudhailer") and with the bland formula he devised to characterise the relationship: his government would "cooperate where we can, disagree where we must and engage in the national interest". Beijing gave Albanese star treatment, including extensive time with President Xi Jinping.

It was as though nothing had ever happened. Australian wine and lobster were back on Chinese banquet tables, and beef in its supermarkets, while Australian cotton was once again on its way to the spinning mills. Chinese students had returned to Australian universities and Australian coal was fuelling Chinese power stations and blast furnaces. Premier Li Qiang and Albanese agreed to review the ten-year-old China–Australia Free Trade Agreement, with China interested in expanding the ecommerce chapter to deal with artificial intelligence.

ECONOMIC ASSAULT

Yet Australia's three years in the Chinese doghouse had resulted in some profound changes. In 2021, the Morrison government struck the AUKUS partnership with the United States and the United Kingdom. The heart of AUKUS is the agreement to provide Australia with nuclear-powered submarines, enabling missions to the South China Sea or the Taiwan Strait, potentially with missiles capable of reaching the Chinese mainland.

The Morrison government injected fresh energy into the "Quad" security partnership with the United States, Japan and India, designed to counter Chinese influence in the Indo-Pacific. It had been largely dormant since 2017 but the four members held joint naval exercises in 2020 and have had regular leaders' summits since 2021.

Australia discovered that its economy was less vulnerable to coercion than either Canberra or Beijing might have anticipated. Australian exporters were, for the most part, able to diversify their markets.

Australian metallurgical coal sales to China's steel mills previously set the benchmark price for the world. And yet when those sales dropped to zero, markets adjusted. China started buying inferior-quality Russian, Mongolian and US coal, and Australia lifted its exports to the markets they had previously serviced, including Europe and India. Analysts believe Chinese steel mills continued sourcing Australian coal through third parties. Barley producers, cotton growers, winemakers and woodchip mills similarly found other buyers. The lobster trade was the worst hit, as it sold most of its output to China. After bans were imposed, lobster exports to Hong Kong surged, with the assumption that they were then being smuggled into China.

For the Australian economy as a whole, China's trade bans did not register. Australia's exports to both China and the world were running at record levels through much of 2021 and 2022 because of soaring commodity prices. At the peak, the bans shut about $20 billion a year of goods from the Chinese market, but exports there were still running at $160 billion a year. The government came under surprisingly little open political pressure from business lobbies to negotiate a peace deal with China. China's decision to drop its trade bans was as unilateral as their imposition, with nothing gained other than the coincidental election in Australia of a government prepared to moderate its rhetoric.

Concern about the depth of Australia's economic engagement with China has been shared by successive US administrations

While the political and economic pain had been manageable, Australia learned that Chinese authorities were prepared to attack its trade, and that the provisions of the China–Australia Free Trade Agreement were not worth the paper they were written on when the Chinese government decided otherwise. They also learned that China was prepared to endure some economic pain to pursue a political point: the ban on Australian coal risked damage to blast furnaces, contributed to power shortages and, until markets adjusted, was costing China's steel mills and power stations sums in the billions of dollars a week. China's brewers had a strong preference for Australian barley and lobbied to have the punitive tariffs removed.

Australia's resilience was hailed as a victory. *The Economist* commented: "Like a surfer surviving a shark attack with no more than a lightly gnawed board, Australia is now emerging from three years of Chinese bullying in remarkably good shape."

And yet the spectacle of the prime minister and an entourage of chief executives drumming up fresh Chinese business after their country had been subjected to a three-year economic assault caused some unease. Australian Strategic Policy Institute executive director Justin Bassi wrote:

> China's unfair trade measures against Australia have indeed ceased, but its broader strategy of compulsion is unchanged. It is still applying pressure through implicit coercive threats, military intimidation and exploitation of political and economic vulnerabilities. We've stabilised just a part of our relations with an aggressor that shows no sign of backing down in its aggression.

An analogy can be drawn with Germany's embrace of Russian energy supplies: even after Russia's annexation of Crimea in 2014, Germany pressed ahead with a massive gas pipeline project. The belief that economic interdependence lessened the prospect of Russian aggression proved unfounded.

Concern about the depth of Australia's economic engagement with China has been shared by successive US administrations. Former treasurer and US ambassador Joe Hockey recalled in his memoir that in 2015, as the relationship between the United States and China was deteriorating, President Barack Obama asked Prime Minister Tony Abbott to stop selling iron ore to China. "Both the prime minister and I were astounded," Hockey said, adding that the sales were critical to the economy and the federal and West Australian budgets.

Current US Secretary of Defense Pete Hegseth underlined his misgivings about allies trading with China in an address to the Shangri-La Dialogue in May:

> We know that many countries are tempted by the idea of seeking both economic cooperation with China and defence cooperation with the United States. Now that is a geographic necessity for many. But beware the leverage that the CCP [Chinese Communist Party] seeks with that entanglement. Economic dependence on China only deepens their malign influence and complicates our defence decision space during times of tension.

Similar concerns had been expressed in private by senior foreign policy and security officials in the Biden administration.

Security strategists want Australia to seek markets elsewhere. "Diversifying away from the one big China market to several smaller markets is plain hard work, and it turns out both the federal government and Australian businesses prefer the easy path," wrote Michael Shoebridge, director of security think-tank Strategic Analysis, as Albanese was in China. Even Albanese, on his Chinese tour, said he wanted to see diversification of Australia's trade beyond China.

However, there has been no sign of it. China's share of Australia's exports has recovered from a low of 29 per cent in 2022 to 35 per cent in 2024, while its share of imports has dropped only marginally from 28 per cent to 26 per cent. Exports to China were more than three times the levels of next-ranked Japan, while imports were more than double those from the United States. The last time Australia had such a lop-sided trade relationship was with the "mother country", England, in the 1950s.

THE RESOURCES BOOM

Two decades of feeding China's appetite for resources has irreversibly reshaped the Australian economy.

The Australian mining industry had grown since the 1960s on the back of Japanese demand, but from 2004 a boom took hold amid an explosion of Chinese demand for raw materials to supply its factories and build its cities and infrastructure.

Andrew "Twiggy" Forrest and Gina Rinehart became overnight billionaires, while global oil giants were building $50-billion liquefied natural gas (LNG) plants, the largest industrial facilities Australia had ever seen. There were huge corporate tussles as BHP and Chinese state-owned miner Chinalco fought for control of Rio Tinto, and bitter iron ore price contract disputes that led to Rio Tinto's negotiating team being thrown into a Chinese jail. When seen from the remote eastern capitals, it was like the Wild West – but Australian travellers abroad thought they'd hit the jackpot when the value of the Australian dollar surged past parity with the US dollar, peaking at US$1.10 in 2011.

Two decades after the excitement began, Australia's economy has been transformed. The resources sector grew from 4 per cent of Australia's GDP in 2004 to peak at 14 per cent in 2023, before dropping back as commodity prices softened to 11.5 per cent in 2024. Manufacturing, which was hit by the exchange rate and the shift of investment capital to the more profitable resources sector, has contracted over the same period from 11 per cent to 5.5 per cent of the economy.

The Australian Bureau of Statistics divides the economy into twenty different industries. In 2004, mining was ranked eleventh, meaning it was smaller than education and a bit bigger than media and communications. Manufacturing was easily the largest sector. Today, mining trumps all others, while manufacturing ranks seventh, between the finance industry and the public sector. No other advanced nation (except for oil-rich Norway) has a

Two decades of feeding China's appetite for resources has irreversibly reshaped the Australian economy

resources sector so large, nor a manufacturing sector so small. The World Bank keeps data on manufacturing as a share of global economies: Australia ranks 151st, between Samoa and Eritrea. There has been a profound change in the structure of the Australian economy.

Australia has become the unrivalled giant of global resources production. It is the largest producer of iron ore, gold, lithium and bauxite. It is the biggest exporter of coal and the third-largest exporter of LNG. It has the biggest deposits of uranium, the second-largest for nickel and the third-largest for copper. Australia's earnings from resources rival Saudi Arabia's earnings from oil and gas. Last year, almost a billion tonnes of Australian mineral ore and coal were loaded onto huge bulk carriers and shipped to China. The Pilbara iron ore mines are the biggest earthmoving operation the world has ever seen.

The resources workforce has jumped from 80,000 to 280,000, while the much bigger manufacturing workforce has dropped by a similar 200,000 to 860,000. But the change has not been limited to those two sectors. Jobs have been created elsewhere, particularly in services that are not vulnerable to international competition. Healthcare has seen the biggest growth, but construction, professional services, education and utilities have all at least doubled their workforce over the past two decades, during which time the total national workforce rose by only 50 per cent.

The impact of a resources boom on a nation's economic structure is well known to economists and has been dubbed the "Dutch disease", after the contraction of manufacturing in the Netherlands following the opening of natural gas fields in the late 1950s. In Australia, seminal research on the phenomenon was published in the mid-1970s by the Australian National University's Professor Bob Gregory.

A booming resources sector will push up the exchange rate, damaging manufacturing businesses that are trying to export or compete with imports. However, it will also bring gains in services sectors that are not internationally traded. The link between rising Chinese demand for Australian resources and the growth of, for example, Australia's healthcare sector is not obvious, but that is how people and governments are spending their Chinese-derived wealth.

There is a sense that the Australian economy has become integrated with China's: when China's economy softens, so does Australia's

The enormous profitability China has delivered to Australia's resources sector has translated to gains in living standards across the nation. Among nations with populations greater than 10 million, Australia's national income per person – a rough indicator of living standard – is the second-highest, after that of the United States. Benefits from the resources sector flow directly through tax payments to the Commonwealth, royalties to states, salaries to staff, contract payments to suppliers and dividend payments to shareholders, including superannuation funds. An indirect gain is that the exchange rate for the Australian dollar is higher than it would otherwise be, and that lowers the cost of imported goods and services for everyone.

Since 2004, when the resources boom got going, the insatiable Chinese demand for our resources has supercharged their prices, while the efficiency of China's massive manufacturing sector has helped cut the average price of our imports. This increase in prices for our exports relative to the declining prices for manufactured imports has translated into a flow of an additional $190 billion a year into the Australian economy. About $60 billion of that winds up with the Commonwealth government through taxes. This flow of tax revenue is how governments have been able to lower deficits, even recording several surpluses, despite lavishing about 2 per cent of GDP on the new National Disability Insurance Scheme.

For most nations, gains in living standards only come from improved productivity: becoming smarter so that more value is generated from the same inputs of labour and capital. That was Australia's experience in the 1990s, when the benefit of far-reaching reforms since the early 1980s to industrial relations, tax, tariffs and competition policy resulted in a surge in productivity growth surpassing that of the United States.

Economic reforms that would deliver productivity gains have become much harder to achieve in Australia, and among most comparable nations, over the last twenty-five years. Some previous reforms, such as floating the dollar, can only be done once, while others – such as increasing the rate of the GST and cutting company taxes to boost investment – would be politically difficult. For many, the result has been stagnation in living standards, which at least partially explains the rise of the extreme right in Europe and the isolationism that motivated Brexit.

But for Australia, the meteoric prices China has paid for minerals have offset the lack of productivity growth. After allowing for inflation and tax, incomes rose by a little under 50 per cent between 2000 and 2025. Just over half that increase came from improved productivity – generating more value for every hour worked – while the remainder came from the increase in prices paid for Australia's exports, relative to the prices we paid for imports.

Export prices have started falling over the last three years in response to weakness in the Chinese economy, though they remain at levels that would have been records at any point in Australia's history prior to the resources boom. The falls have translated to modest reductions in Australian living standards. Australians still stand near the top of the global rankings for both income and wealth, but there is a sense that the Australian economy has become integrated with China's: when China's economy softens, so does Australia's.

MANUFACTURING WOES

Labor leader Kevin Rudd declared in the lead-up to the 2007 federal election that he did not want to be prime minister of a country that doesn't make things, yet his first year in office marked the high point for Australian manufacturing. Manufacturing as a share of the economy has been declining in most developed countries since the 1970s, but from 2008 Australian manufacturing output has been falling in absolute terms.

The motor industry was the highest-profile closure. Ford, Toyota and General Motors decided in 2013 and 2014 that they could not profitably continue manufacturing in Australia. At the time of its closure, the Australian motor industry ranked as the thirtieth-largest in the world, behind that of Uzbekistan, so it lacked scale. And with the Australian dollar still above 80 US cents, it could not compete with imports or export profitably to the markets it was trying to forge in the Middle East.

Other closures were legion. They included factories making whitegoods, tyres, tinned soup, sports clothing and building materials. Factories making wind turbines and solar panels shut. Aside from the factories making goods for consumers, those making inputs – such as petrochemical and plastics plants, aluminium rolling mills and steel pipe mills – also closed.

There are other contributors to the decline of Australian manufacturing besides Chinese competition and the exchange rate. A lack of scale and distance from international markets and suppliers means Australian factories are not linked to the value chains that drive global manufacturing. High labour and energy costs compound these problems. And the lack of competitiveness in manufacturing compared with the super profits from resources means it is starved of investment capital.

The Australian dollar has dropped back since the early 2010s but is still about 25 per cent higher, on a trade-weighted basis, than it was in the years before the resources boom got underway. The pressure on manufacturing continues.

The Albanese government came to office in 2022 promising a manufacturing revival based on renewable energy and innovation but has found itself fighting rearguard actions to save the Whyalla steel mill and a series of smelters and refineries making aluminium, lead, zinc and copper metals. Metals prices have been good but the margin for turning mineral ores into metal has been whittled away to nothing by Chinese competitors and Australia's energy and labour costs. China's relatively modern metals processing capacity is more efficient than Australia's, much of which dates from the 1960s. Because China has built more capacity than its own market can absorb, its smelters receive government subsidies to make sure their exports can beat their competition.

As Australia's manufacturing capacity has dwindled, its dependence on imports, particularly from China, has grown. An Australia Institute report found that Australia had the lowest self-sufficiency in manufacturing in the Organisation for Economic Co-operation and Development. Imports supplied almost half of domestic consumption of manufactured goods, placing Australia at the bottom of advanced-country rankings.

China supplies 32 per cent of Australia's manufactured imports, which is about double China's share of global manufactured goods trade. A sample of items where China has much larger shares of Australia's imports includes lighting (80 per cent), steel and aluminium structures (70 per cent), integrated circuits (65 per cent), telecommunications and office equipment (60 per cent), footwear, clothing and textiles (55 per cent) and chemicals (40 per cent). Sectors heavily dependent on China include retail, construction, chemicals, telecommunications and transport.

BOUND TO EACH OTHER

A succession of Australian governments has supported the economic relationship with China. Even before diplomatic relations were established by the Whitlam government in 1974, the Menzies government defied a US embargo to open Australia's wheat trade with China in the early 1960s and removed the pre-war ban on iron exports. The Hawke government facilitated China's first foreign direct investment in an iron ore joint venture with Rio Tinto, while Prime Minister John Howard secured Australia's gas market in China, signing a twenty-five-year contract for Woodside.

However, the surge in Australia's trade with China over the past twenty years was not the result of government policy. Rather, it resulted from the ability of the resource companies to respond to the incredible surge in Chinese demand. Where Australia's iron ore production rose more than 400 per cent between 2000 and 2020, its chief rival, Brazil, was only able to lift output by 90 per cent. There was no deliberate choice: Australia's economy became integrated with China's – its resource sector multiplying in size as its manufacturing shrank – in response to profound economic forces.

That integration is evident in the conveyor belt of several hundred super bulk carriers constantly running between the ports of the Pilbara and China to keep the steel mills supplied. An amazing 63 per cent of Australia's export shipping tonnage is destined for China.

Defence minister Richard Marles has justified the acquisition of nuclear-powered submarines, saying that while Australia is not at risk of invasion, the purpose of the submarines would be "to resist the coercion that would come from the disruption of our sea lines of communication". However, Australia's most important sea line is that running through the Indonesian archipelago and the South China Sea to Qingdao, Dalian and the other major Chinese ports.

China did not target Australia's iron ore during its coercive campaign because it has no alternative

China did not target Australia's iron ore during its coercive campaign because it has no alternative. Australian iron ore supported the production of about half of China's steel output in 2024, up from less than a third in 2012. China's own domestic iron ore production has been falling as high-cost mines are shut down. This has made China more dependent on imports, of which Australia is providing a larger share.

The new Simandou mine in Guinea being brought into production by Rio Tinto and Chinese joint ventures is high-quality and will have a damaging effect on price, but it will only be about an eighth the size of the Pilbara's combined production. It will not materially reduce China's dependence on Australia. The Productivity Commission has commented that the interdependence lessens the risk of "geopolitically inspired disruptions" as both economies have a vested interest in the efficient functioning of the market.

The changes in the Australian economy wrought by the force of Chinese demand cannot be undone by government fiat. There have been big changes in Australia's markets in the past, as is shown by the replacement of the United Kingdom as our primary trading partner by Japan and then China. However, the resources sector is umbilically bound to the Chinese market for the foreseeable future.

While great hopes are held for critical minerals such as lithium and rare earths, these sectors are small relative to iron ore. The Department of Industry expects that new critical minerals projects will add less than $4 billion to Australia's exports by 2030. And China remains the primary market, last year taking 95 per cent of Australia's lithium exports.

China's growth is slowing, while India and South-East Asia continue to expand, yet Australia's exports to China are seven times bigger than to India, and almost three times larger than to South-East Asia. Changes in relative growth rates will do no more than nibble at those margins.

The manufacturers who have gone will not return. Government efforts to encourage a revival may support some individual businesses but will not reverse the slow erosion of the sector, nor Australia's dependence on imported manufactured goods.

THE CATASTROPHE OF CONFLICT

A war between China and the United States, whether over Taiwan or anything else, would be catastrophic for the global economy. The two countries briefly considered the prospect of severing their bilateral trade in April 2025, when the United States raised tariffs on Chinese goods to 145 per cent and China reciprocated with 125 per cent barriers. They soon backed down – on the American side, the major retailers warned of empty shelves and a bleak Christmas, while manufacturers, led by the car industry, warned of shutdowns because they couldn't source rare earth magnets.

For Australia, the impact would be much worse. In addition to the loss of all trade with China, trade with other Asian partners would be hit. North and South-East Asia collectively take 81 per cent of Australia's maritime exports and supply 66 per cent of imports by value. A conflict over Taiwan would threaten shipping routes to Japan, Korea and, of course, Taiwan, while a conflict in the South China Sea would threaten the routes to South-East Asia and Korea.

Australia's maritime trade, 2023–24

	Exports	Imports
China	$190 billion	$91 billion
Other East Asia	$130 billion	$61 billion
South-East Asia	$61 billion	$71 billion
South Asia	$24 billion	$11 billion
Europe	$16 billion	$52 billion
North America	$16 billion	$33 billion
Rest of world	$30 billion	$19 billion
Total	**$467 billion**	**$338 billion**

Source: BITRE

About two-thirds of Australia's maritime exports and 40 per cent of imports by value travel through the Indonesian archipelago, including most trade with the Middle East and Europe. A further 25 per cent of maritime exports and 40 per cent of imports are traded with North Asia, travelling into the North Pacific via the east coast of Papua New Guinea. Virtually the entirety of Australia's liquid fuel imports traverses these routes, which would be highly vulnerable in a war. Australia owns no international shipping and would depend on global shipping lines continuing to service its needs in wartime.

In 2018, the Department of Defence conducted a workshop with industry association Engineers Australia to explore a scenario in which a collapse of global governance led to the cessation of Australia's international trade. The results, released in response to a freedom-of-information request, pointed to rapid social breakdown. Mass layoffs would begin within a week. By two months, liquid fuel would be almost exhausted and food shortages would be emerging. By three months, transport would have ceased, and services dependent on imported spares, such as electricity and telecommunications, would begin degrading.

History shows that trade does not stop during wars, so the scenario is too extreme. To cite current examples, Ukraine has maintained trade through the Black Sea in the face of Russian attacks, while Houthi assaults on shipping through the Red Sea have slowed but not stopped the flow of ships traversing the Suez Canal. Some liquid fuel and other supplies would still get through, but the loss of Australia's trade with China and the likely extension of a conflict zone to other principal Asian trading partners would cause inescapable hardship and social stress.

The 1987 Defence White Paper, prepared when Kim Beazley was defence minister and articulating a strategy of "self-reliance", commented that "Australia enjoys a high degree of economic self-sufficiency. We are a net exporter of energy and self-sufficient in food." It went on to note that "Australia could survive significant disruption of overseas trade in the event of global war".

That is no longer the case. Australia is still self-sufficient in food, but depends on imports from China for the packaging, without which much food cannot be sold. It depends on imports for 85 per cent of its refined liquid fuel products. The COVID-19 pandemic highlighted the sometimes-random nature of disruptions. Shortages of the fuel additive AdBlue threatened to stop the trucking industry, while shortages of stone-cutting tools threatened the quarries essential to making concrete. China has a lock on the global market for ceramic toilets and basins, without which no home, office, warehouse or factory can be built.

Three decades of globalisation have made Australia, like most nations, much more dependent on trade. Trade now represents 44 per cent of Australia's GDP, up from 33 per cent in the mid-1980s. Autarky is not an option.

MANAGING THE FUDGE

Reflecting on his successful relations with both China and the United States, John Howard remarked in 2017: "I hope Australian leaders are not seduced into this stupid argument that some advance, that we've got to make a choice between China and the United States. I can't think of anything more ridiculous. It's in our interest to have close relations with both of those countries."

The reality is that choices between Australia's economic welfare and security interests are a constant. When the Turnbull government barred Huawei from supplying infrastructure for Australia's 5G mobile network, it consciously rejected the cheapest, fastest and technically superior option because of advice that the security risks associated with a Chinese company could not be mitigated. When successive governments rejected Chinese foreign investment proposals to acquire rare earths deposits or critical infrastructure, they chose security over economic benefit. The Albanese government's resolve to terminate the lease held by Chinese company Landbridge over Port Darwin, could be seen as the expropriation by government of a legally acquired Chinese asset on grounds of security.

In the near future, Australian governments will face decisions over Chinese-supplied artificial intelligence services and the collection of data from Chinese electric vehicles, which have been described as mobile listening devices. When making these calls, governments will have to weigh the risk of Chinese economic retaliation against national security arguments.

Despite the bonhomie of Albanese's trip last year, the Chinese government remains acutely aware of Australia's security posture. After the Australian military conducted extensive exercises in the Philippines with local and US armed forces last August, the state-run *China Daily* editorialised that Australia wanted to "butter both sides of its bread at the same time" by benefiting from trade with China at the same time as engaging in AUKUS, which it said was targeting China, and supporting the Philippines in the South China Sea.

"Although China attaches importance to economic and trade relations with Australia, it will under no circumstances tolerate such infringements of its core interests," the newspaper said. Australia's "two-faced policy toward China" was "not sustainable in the long run".

The Chinese government remains acutely aware of Australia's security posture

Australia is more dependent on China as a market for its exports than any other country, except for small bordering states such as Laos and Mongolia. Even Russia, which turned to China after losing much of its European export market, sends a smaller share of its exports to the Chinese market than Australia.

There has been a global trend for countries to increase the share of their trade that is conducted with countries that are their geopolitical allies. The International Monetary Fund has spoken of the global trade solidifying into three blocs: one centred on China, one on the United States and a third non-aligned. Australia gets put into the US bloc in such speculations, although the United States takes less than 5 per cent of Australia's goods exports.

A recent study by the Bank for International Settlements – the Swiss-based central bank for the world's central banks – looked at trading patterns among countries, according to their "geopolitical distance", which it measured by counting how often countries voted with each other at United Nations General Assembly meetings. China and the United States were at opposite extremes, with Australia's voting record very close to that of the United States. Between 2017 and 2023, it found, trade between geopolitical allies grew 10 per cent a year faster than between adversaries.

The share of Australia's exports going to fellow advanced nations rose to a twelve-year high of 41 per cent in 2022, the peak year for China's export bans, led by a surge in sales to Japan and South Korea, but it has since dropped back to a record low of 35 per cent. The share of imports coming from advanced nations, which as recently as 2017 was at 52 per cent, has dropped to 44 per cent, which is close to a record low.

The BIS study also looked at the difficulty in diversifying trade. When an adversary accounts for a large share of global demand, it is impossible to diversify exports. There were countries with a larger share of their exports going to adversaries: China topped the list. However, no country faced a greater impediment to diversification of exports than Australia.

Australia is an outlier: it has more of its trade tied to China than any other advanced nation; it is not increasing its trade with geopolitically aligned countries, and it has less opportunity to diversify its trade away from a geopolitical adversary than any other country. Australia cannot escape the gravitational pull of the Chinese economy. It is caught and will remain in its orbit. Navigating the tensions between economic prosperity and national security, with the ever-attendant risk of economic coercion from its superpower trading partner, will be the lot of many Australian governments to come. ■

STAYING OPEN

How to counter Trump's great disruption

MELISSA CONLEY TYLER

In 1900, as Australia was preparing to become a nation, trade was a central issue. Frustration with the high tariffs and duties imposed on trade between the colonies was an important driver of federation. The Free Trade Party triumphed when Australia became a single market, with the constitution guaranteeing that trade and commerce within Australia shall be absolutely free. Yet the first parliament would be dominated by the Protectionists with a platform of using tariffs to limit cheap overseas imports. Australia was born with a high tariff wall around the country, and free trade within.

In the 1980s, this shifted dramatically. Australia slashed tariffs and became one of the most free-trading nations on Earth. This delivered decades of economic growth – and built broad support for trade. In the 2024 Lowy Poll, 77 per cent of Australians said free trade was good for the economy and 80 per cent that it was good for their standard of living; 90 per cent also said that a culturally diverse population has been positive for Australia, showing support for the movement of people as well as the free flow of goods.

Today, open global trade is under assault. Australia had weathered Chinese trade restrictions only to be hit by the economic shocks from the United States' protectionist policies. Australia's security ally is now undermining the open global trade on which it built its prosperity.

This is confronting for Australia. However, shellshocked as it may be, Australia still has agency. It needs to understand its assets and its vulnerabilities and to learn from what has worked.

—

Trade wars are never just about trade. Trade is about the sort of society we want to be.

In 1900, Australians discussed trade in the context of class, with a vision of providing decent jobs – "a working man's paradise" – in a new egalitarian nation. They also discussed it in the context of race, protecting a "White Australia" from foreign goods and foreign labour. In their more febrile moments, some dreamt that the country might become a manufacturing powerhouse to rival the United States and Europe, with tariffs nurturing home-grown industries. When the Hawke and Keating governments changed direction and slashed tariffs in the 1980s, it was to avoid becoming a third-world "banana republic" economy.

Today, President Donald Trump uses trade wars to show his supporters that he is doing something about rusted-out factories and hollowed-out communities. Where jobs and livelihoods have gone, this has led to a loss of self-worth – and the availability of cheaper goods does not compensate for this. When Trump says that other countries are "ripping off" the United States, his supporters hear him fighting to protect a way of life.

Yet Trump's trade wars look more like performance than a serious attempt at redistribution. It is easy to mobilise grievance through narratives that attack international trade and foreign workers for "stealing jobs". It is certainly easier than challenging the models of capitalism and government that have allowed these communities of despair to come into being. Trade brings aggregate gains for a country. It is then a political decision how these gains are distributed, both geographically and among different socio-economic groups.

Of course, the challenges to open trade are not just coming from the Trump administration. China has repeatedly used trade restrictions as a tool to demonstrate its displeasure with other countries. Justifiably, trade sanctions have been used by the international community in response to Russia's invasion of Ukraine. These tactics can be termed "economic statecraft" – the use of economic instruments to achieve foreign policy objectives. Even countries that haven't

Today, all three pillars of Australia's security and prosperity are crumbling

embraced tariffs are using tools such as industry policy to strengthen specific industries for geostrategic purposes.

Having to deal with economic statecraft is not a new challenge for Australia. What is new is the scale of the disruption and the actor causing it.

—

Openness to trade has been an important part of Australian foreign policy over recent decades. What have been described as the three pillars of Australia's security and prosperity – our relationship with the United States, our close engagement with Asia, and our reliance on global rules – have all supported trade. We have had a great and powerful friend that (at least rhetorically) supported open trade, trade-oriented neighbours in a fast-growing part of the world, and international rules and institutions facilitating trade.

Australia has reaped the benefits of this approach. It still holds the record for the longest period of uninterrupted economic growth by a developed country. For twenty-nine years until the COVID-19 pandemic, Australia avoided recession during a turbulent period that included the Asian financial crisis, the collapse of the dotcom bubble and the global financial crisis. This period of growth, fuelled by trade, increased Australians' household income and standards of living. Geographically, all states and territories have benefited.

Today, all three pillars of Australia's security and prosperity are crumbling. First, the United States is a different partner than it once was. While there has always been a gap between what Australia wanted the United States to be and the reality, it is now a chasm. The Trump administration has imposed tariffs that are flagrantly in breach of trade agreements it has signed – including the Australia–United States Free Trade Agreement. Second, Asia's economic growth trajectory is threatened, with the potential for significant impact on prosperity and stability in the region. Third, international rules and norms are under strain from a variety of actors. There is a sense of international rules being ignored, including the all-important norm prohibiting the use of force across borders. This is a profoundly disturbing time for Australia; but it is not powerless.

There is little that Australia can do about what is happening in US politics and foreign policy during a period that has been described as a "socio-cultural revolution". Australia will have to watch the United States go through its current convulsions and see what it looks like at the other end.

What Australia can do is to work even harder to bolster the other pillars of its security and prosperity: engaging with Asia and promoting international rules.

—

The trade wars hit Asia hard. China was the primary target, given its huge trade deficit with the United States. But this also affected countries that trade with China – which is to say, everyone. Trump's "Liberation Day" tariffs were indiscriminate, falling equally on US allies such as Japan and South Korea and on the penguins of Heard Island.

For low- and middle-income countries in Asia, tariffs were part of a double-whammy. In one of his crueller and more callous acts, Trump signed an executive order the day he was inaugurated ordering a ninety-day pause in US foreign development assistance. The US Agency for International Development (USAID) was ordered to halt funding and was eventually disbanded. Soon after, tariffs hit. Every country has been affected by one or the other. Some, like Cambodia, were affected by both. This has had a huge impact on economic growth trajectories and on human development.

There will be an important role for Australia to engage as a partner to countries in the region. Stepping out of the United States' shadow, Australia can differentiate itself through practical cooperation across the Indo-Pacific, including through its diplomacy, defence cooperation, development program, trade, education and people-to-people links.

Recent initiatives in South-East Asia provide a good example of how Australia can harness its tools of statecraft for greater engagement. On the diplomatic front, Australia now has a Comprehensive Strategic Partnership with ASEAN. Australia's messaging about playing a role in supporting "strategic equilibrium" – where no country dominates and countries are not forced to choose but can make their own sovereign choices – has resonated well with countries in the region. This helped repair some of the damage done by the Morrison government's unexpected announcement of the Australia–United Kingdom–United States (AUKUS) defence procurement agreement, which some viewed as inflaming major power competition. Defence cooperation with countries across the region has been growing steadily, including in maritime security. This was capped in November 2025 by a significant security treaty with Indonesia.

Even when 2025 brought massive cuts to foreign assistance from the largest donors, Australia did not cut its development spending, instead saying that it would remain a steadfast and reliable partner. Policymakers seem to have grasped that vacating the field on development issues would incur unacceptable reputational, diplomatic and strategic costs. Across government, there has been engagement with South-East Asia on issues like climate change, energy, counterterrorism, cyber threats and agriculture. Other policy levers are being used to promote people-to-people ties, such as universities being offered increased international student places if they demonstrate stronger engagement with South-East Asia.

Trade and investment have been a particular area of focus, in line with a blueprint *Southeast Asia Economic Strategy* developed by former Macquarie Group chief executive Nicholas Moore. For decades, trade and investment ties have been the missing link in engagement; even today, Australian companies invest less in the whole of South-East Asia than they do in New Zealand. Given the importance of the region to Australia's prosperity and security, the government is playing a proactive role to facilitate greater trade and investment. There are Investment Deal Teams working with Australian companies to spot opportunities and get them moving. There is a Southeast Asia Business Exchange to help Australian exporters figure out how to enter and compete in these markets. There is a young professionals placement program to build business connections, and an impact investment fund for female entrepreneurs. There is a $2-billion Southeast Asia Investment Financing Facility to reduce risks for investors willing to back projects that align with the Moore Report's priorities.

Tools like this can be used to increase engagement across the region: in the Pacific, the Indian Ocean and East Asia, as well as South-East Asia. The potential impact of the trade wars on the growth and stability of the region should intensify our focus on what we can do, using many tools of statecraft, to engage with and help build a region we want to live in.

—

Multilateral rules and institutions have also been hit hard by the Trump administration. For example, US funding cuts last year led to the United Nations sacking 20 per cent of its staff. The hostility the first Trump administration showed to trade institutions such as the World Trade Organization (WTO) has continued.

In doing what it can to maintain the pillars of its prosperity, Australia can draw on other moments of leadership. During the first Trump administration, the United States shut down the WTO appeals process by refusing to appoint new judges. This meant that cases could no longer be heard and that breaches of international trade rules could no longer be prosecuted. In response, Australia worked with a group of countries to create the Multi-Party Interim Appeal Arbitration Agreement so that there was still some dispute settlement process to enforce international trade laws. Interestingly, it was embraced by a range of countries, including Mexico, Brazil and even China. Australia used this process to force China to remove remaining trade restrictions on lobsters and wine. More broadly, Australia benefited by maintaining the efficacy of the rules-based trading system through access to an independent appeals process for dispute settlement. Today, fifty-seven of the WTO's members have signed up to use this process in trade disputes between one another.

Similarly, when the United States withdrew from the proposed Trans-Pacific Partnership (TPP) during the first Trump administration, other countries, led by Japan, stepped up and concluded negotiations. With Australia's support, the deal went ahead: the renamed Comprehensive and Progressive Agreement for Trans-Pacific Partnership (CPTPP) is now one of the largest free trade agreements in the world, covering 14 per cent of global gross domestic product (GDP). And it is still growing. In 2024, the United Kingdom signed on; China, Taiwan, Indonesia, the Philippines and the United Arab Emirates are in the queue to join. Australia has just held the chair of the CPTPP in 2025. Australia identified three priorities for its hosting year: to make it easier for members to trade with each other, to spread the benefits of trade and also to increase economic gains to communities in each country. In the end, that's what trade is about.

In these times, we need narratives that don't relegate people to the margins

These examples show the potential for multilateralism without the United States. There are even more examples if we go back in history, such as Australia's role in establishing the Cairns Group to bring together agricultural-exporting countries that support fair and free trade as a counter to US and EU agricultural protectionism. Australia played a key role in creating the Asia-Pacific Economic Cooperation (APEC) forum to liberalise trade.

More broadly, a recent example of Australia's leadership in promoting adherence to international law is the Declaration for the Protection of Humanitarian Personnel. Following the death of Australian aid worker Zomi Frankcom in Gaza, Australia gathered a disparate group of countries, including Colombia, Indonesia, Jordan and Sierra Leonne, to develop a declaration that reaffirms nations' obligations under international humanitarian law and that galvanises a commitment to protect those who are risking their lives for others. Thanks to a year-long effort from Australian diplomats and civil society, more than 100 countries signed up when the declaration was launched at the United Nations. It stands as an example of how Australia can find common ground with a wide range of countries even in the absence – indeed, despite the opposition – of the United States.

Australia can draw on these examples to continue to work with other countries to support the rules and institutions that underpin open trade.

—

Alongside the Trump administration's wars on trade, aid and multilateralism is another that is not always recognised: a war on social cohesion. Trump has reaped the benefit of using anti-trade and anti-globalist narratives to differentiate himself from establishment politicians.

Australia is already subject to foreign interference by a range of openly and covertly hostile actors. Documented cases in 2025 include attacks on Australia's Jewish community directed by Iran and influenced by Islamic State, Russian targeting of supporters of Ukraine, and harassment of a community group by the People's Republic of China. The level of polarisation in the United States today adds another risk to Australia's stability. Particularly since it shares the English language, Australia is constantly hit by corrosive American messaging. The level of toxic partisanship imported from the United States makes it harder for Australians to find common cause with each other and to see themselves as a polity. With social division in the United States at historic highs, it would be perilously easy for Australia to follow this path. In some ways, Australia probably looks more stable than it is, given the intergenerational gift of the world's best electoral system. The key elements of Australia's democratic system – including compulsory voting and the preferential ballot – all push towards the centre rather than the extremes.
On other indicators there is cause for concern. For example, the latest

McKinnon Index of democratic health found that around one in ten Australians does not vote, and one in six votes mainly to avoid a fine.

In these times, we need narratives that don't relegate people to the margins. We need systems that support inclusivity. We need debate that acknowledges different perspectives – including from the fringes.

To counter the anti-trade and anti-openness narratives emanating from the United States, Australian leaders need to explain the links between trade and foreign policy and the real impacts they have in people's lives. They need to make the case. Just as the Biden administration pledged to deliver "foreign policy for the middle class" as a way to sell internationalism to economically squeezed Americans, Australian leaders need to link openness to concrete benefits for all – to help combat division.

—

At the local level, what have the trade wars and other disruptions of the last year brought? I've been watching from the New England region, which you may know as Barnaby Joyce's electorate. You might hear his forays into anti-trade rhetoric – such as describing clean energy projects as "foreign intermittent power swindle factories" – and wonder if that's a common view.

Where I live, in Armidale, I see international trade all around. The paddocks are full of exports. Armidale hosts the societies for breeders of Wagyu, Herefords, Lowline cattle, Dorper sheep and others. Local wineries export to markets such as China and Singapore. A huge tomato farm nearby attracts Pacific Australia Labour Mobility Scheme seasonal workers and exports to Asia, North America and Europe.

The University of New England is the biggest employer. Of its 3500 on-campus students, 1200 are international students who have come from over seventy different countries. Many of the secondary schools in the area host international students – including The Armidale School, New England Girls School, Presbyterian Ladies' College and Armidale Secondary College – either as boarders or on homestay.

One of Australia's underestimated skills is our ability to adapt to international shocks

Armidale has a business incubator. There are thriving creative industries – such as the New England Regional Art Museum and the New England Conservatorium of Music – which are part of international networks. Immigration offered Ezidi people from Syria and Iraq a haven and has been swelling the Armidale population, with new arrivals now starting to establish small businesses.

It is part of a renewable energy zone, attracting investment in large-scale clean energy projects as a catalyst for jobs and growth. Contrary to our member of parliament's bugbear, the research shows that there is no statistically significant difference between the opinions of urban and regional Australians on climate change.

The thing that has struck me most is the resilience of the community. During the time I have been here, I've seen the impact of COVID, floods and a snowstorm; I've seen the aftermath of a tornado and drought. A 10 per cent tariff on exports to the United States is the sort of turbulence that people around here are used to dealing with.

But how much is community cohesion at risk? How worried should we be about the US domestic political messages that have led to the trade wars taking hold? In the last election, Trumpet of Patriots, Pauline Hanson's One Nation and Family First together received 16 per cent of the vote in the New England electorate. Barnaby Joyce has now joined One Nation. This suggests there is some reservoir for those who wish to cultivate social division to reap political benefits.

People in rural and remote areas generally have lower incomes, worse health outcomes and less access to services than residents of big cities. The larger the gap between groups, such asbetween the cities and the regions, the more risk it creates for Australia.

If we want to avoid the divisions that have led to Trump's trade wars, we must commit to policies that genuinely benefit the people who feel least connected to the nation. There is no reason for rural people without basic dental care to support open trade for economic growth that never trickles down. The privileged – which includes most of the people reading this article – have to see their own long-term self-interest in sharing some of their spoils.

So, as well as engaging with Asia and protecting the international system, Australia needs to focus on the strength of its society at home. Like Trump, Australia needs to use foreign policy for domestic ends. Unlike Trump's polarising narratives, though, we need to find a foreign policy that brings Australians together.

—

In a time of trade wars, what assets do Australians have? We have a continent and, thanks to federation, a single economy. We have immediate neighbours that aren't our enemies. We have serious defence capabilities that deter aggression. We produce things that people want – healthy food, education and resources for the world's energy needs, both for today and into the future.

We have institutions of good government. We have political stability, enjoying 125 years without a major change in our constitutional system – something hardly any other country can boast. Much of the population is well educated, informed and outward-looking. We are a lifestyle superpower, which gives us an advantage in attracting international talent, including in the technology innovation that has become a key battleground for national success. If we stay open to trade, migration and ideas, we can reap the benefits.

Internationally, we are joiners. We want to work with others. It's easy to take this for granted but it is rarer than you might think. In a time of unilateralism – whether by Trump, Putin or Xi – this is a real asset. Australia can work with its close neighbours, which also see trade as a lifeblood. We can work with similarly positioned countries anywhere to maintain what we can of international norms and rules.

In that sense, Australia remains lucky. There are many worse places to be. Talking about the trade wars, former minister for trade

Simon Birmingham reminds that Australians "are fortunate to still be in the best region of the world. Asia seems determined not to be drawn into this vortex and to stay open."

One of Australia's underestimated skills is our ability to adapt to international shocks. It was a huge shock to the economy when the United Kingdom joined the European Common Market in 1973 and Australia's exporters lost their duty-free entry to the British market. But Australia adapted and accelerated the process of trade integration with its region. When China imposed trade restrictions on Australia earlier this decade, Australian exporters in all but a few of the most exposed sectors were able to pivot quickly and successfully to other markets.

Australia might lack a grand strategy – which means that its resilience can look like dumb luck – but our ability to respond to change quickly and unsentimentally is also an asset. In that sense, Trump has done Australians a favour by forcing us to confront the ways in which the world is changing and the need for a strategy that suits the times.

At the start of its next 125 years, Australia's biggest vulnerability is the fabric of our society. In a time when grievance and intolerance are supercharged by technology, the normalisation of inflammatory rhetoric – exemplified by Trump's trade wars – challenges our cohesion. That means our foreign policy needs to work in two directions. Outwardly, it needs to shore up the pillars of our success: norms and rules, Asia engagement and as good a relationship with the United States as is currently possible. Inwardly, it needs to bring us together. By presenting a clear statement on who we are internationally, we can help keep a sense of ourselves at home.

As foreign minister, Penny Wong has been weaving a narrative that includes both directions. As she puts it, "This is what success looks like for me. A stronger and more influential Australia. Connected in our region and respected in the world. Where we know who we are, what we want, and where we are going – together."

That's the challenge. At a time when US domestic divisions have led to global disruption, we need a foreign policy that binds us rather than divides. ■

BUYING POWER

An economic playbook for the era of Trump and Xi

RICHARD HOLDEN

Three decades ago, the North American Free Trade Agreement (NAFTA) came into effect. It was originally signed by a Republican president, George Herbert Walker Bush, in late 1992. And it was a Democratic president, Bill Clinton, who shepherded it through the US Congress and signed it into law in December 1993.

In the two decades that followed, globalisation reigned. During that period, the US economy grew by two-thirds. China's GDP more than quadrupled. There was, if only for a time, a seemingly universal consensus that free trade was better for rich countries and for poor countries. In the words of Aaron Sorkin (via Toby Ziegler) in *The West Wing*: "You want the benefits of free trade? Food is cheaper. Clothes are cheaper. Steel is cheaper. Cars are cheaper. Phone service is cheaper ... It lowers prices. It raises incomes ... Free trade stops wars."

The first inklings that this era might come to an end emerged in 2017. In January, Donald Trump took the oath of office as President of the United States. Trump's election was, in some ways, the culmination of a backlash against globalisation from those communities in the United States who had seen few of the upsides and suffered most of the downsides of free trade. In Trump, Americans who longed for an easier time found not only a fierce advocate but a president who had a long history of hostility towards free trade and a fondness for tariffs. In October 2017, meanwhile, Xi Jinping was reappointed as General Secretary of the Chinese Communist Party, which marked the beginning of the end of presidential term limits in China (ratified in 2018) and the adoption of "Xi Jinping Thought" into the text of the CCP's constitution.

It didn't happen immediately, but these men would fundamentally change the world economic order. Xi consolidated his grip on power, and when Trump, who had been voted out in late 2020, was re-elected in 2024, the era of globalisation and free trade gave way to an awkward hybrid system in which nation-states play a dramatically larger role in the global economy. This was a return not just to industrial policy interventionism but to the use of state power to fundamentally affect economic outcomes.

In the era of globalisation, all that mattered was *comparative advantage*: what a country was relatively better at than other countries. This era was marked not only by extraordinary innovations such as the personal computer, the smartphone and new pharmaceuticals but also by their spread around the world – at least for people who could afford them.

In the Trump–Xi era, it's not that comparative advantage doesn't matter anymore. It does. But it's not the only thing that matters. In this new era, *leverage* has become fundamentally important. And leverage comes in two forms: offensive and defensive. The United States under Trump has offensive leverage – and hence can impose tariffs – for a reason that Trump himself often emphasises: the US is a really big market, and many companies simply can't afford not to sell into it. Similarly, China has leverage because of the size of its market. It can, for instance, cut off Australian exports of lobster and barley to get (some of) what it wants from Australia, both economically and politically.

But defensive leverage is also critical. Having something that a country exercising offensive leverage wants is a kind of antidote to that power. A good example of this is Australia and critical minerals. Prime Minister Anthony Albanese had a valuable bargaining chip with Trump because of the importance of critical minerals to the US economy and Australia's abundance of them.

In the Trump–Xi era, leverage has become fundamentally important

There's an important caveat to both forms of leverage: timeframe. It's one thing for a country to need something; it's another thing for the country to need something *now*. The longer a country can go without something, the more time it has to adjust, and hence the less power other countries have over it. This is an important part of thinking about who has leverage and how much they have. It's important for thinking about government policy. Having the time to adjust doesn't matter much if the adjustment can't be made. So the policy areas for a country to prioritise are those in which another country has a lot of leverage but in which you can make an effective adjustment.

If that was a description of what has happened, it's a prologue to thinking about what this new global order means for countries including (but by no means limited to) Australia, and what policy options are best for adapting. That's the subject of the rest of this essay. But here's where it's going.

As a kind of warm-up, consider the trade-off between firms and markets within a closed economy with no international trade. What's good about firms is that they can make use of their authority. If I'm making cars and I want them painted green, then within my firm I can just make that happen. I tell my people to paint them green – and if they don't, I fire them and find new people who will paint them green. That's better than what happens in an arms-length market exchange, where I can't tell the other party what to do and have to haggle with them.

But what's bad about firms is that they don't make use of the market's price mechanism, whereby prices are set through the interaction of supply and demand. They miss the magic of the market emphasised in 1945 by economist Friedrich Hayek. Presciently, Hayek observed that the price mechanism drastically reduces the information demands required to coordinate economic activity. Prices are a sufficient statistic for the information that households and firms need to make optimal consumption and production decisions.

If firms and markets can sometimes be better or worse than each other, then there's an important trade-off to analyse. In a 2012 *Quarterly Journal of Economics* paper with Bob Gibbons and Mike Powell, I did just that. We showed formally (that is, mathematically) how firms and markets are alternative ways of organising economic activity, but also how they interact with and shape each other. So in a sense economists already understand the benefits and drawbacks of firms and markets *within* an economy. The purpose of this essay is to sketch an approach to extending that to involve international trade. This involves replacing the CEO of a firm with the nation-state, and replacing the price mechanism with the fundamental component of international trade: comparative advantage.

COMPARATIVE ADVANTAGE

Comparative advantage is the idea that countries benefit from trade rather than seeking to produce everything they need locally. The idea was first articulated by David Ricardo in his 1817 book *On the Principles of Political Economy and Taxation.*

One country (let's call it Country A) might be more efficient than another (Country B) at producing, for example, T-shirts and wine. It is tempting to think, then, that Country A should produce both T-shirts and wine. But what if Country B is really inefficient at producing T-shirts but reasonable at producing wine? If Country A specialises in producing T-shirts and Country B specialises in producing wine, they can trade and both be better off.

Why? Because Country A produces T-shirts much more efficiently than Country B, and Country B is only a little less efficient at producing wine. Overall, both economies become more efficient, raising living standards.

There's not much more to it than that, but the concept of comparative advantage has far-reaching implications. Which is perhaps why the great economist Paul Samuelson observed in 1969: "That it is logically true need not be argued before a mathematician; that it is not trivial is attested by the thousands of important and intelligent men who have never been able to grasp the doctrine for themselves or to believe it after it was explained to them."

The question of where comparative advantage comes from, however, remains open. Why do some countries have a comparative advantage in some sectors and not in others?

In 1933, economist Bertil Ohlin expanded on the earlier work of political economist Eli Heckscher to publish what is now commonly known as the Heckscher–Ohlin model. The basic idea is that countries export goods that intensively use the factors of production they have in abundance, while they import goods that intensively use factors they have in scarcity.

This means that a country with a lot of labour relative to capital (say, Bangladesh) will export labour-intensive goods (such as textiles). On the other hand, a country with abundant capital relative to labour (say, Germany) will export capital-intensive goods (such as cars and products involving advanced manufacturing).

It's important to note that there are more modern theories of international trade. Among them is Paul Krugman's Nobel Prize–winning contribution known as the "new trade theory", which emphasises economies of scale. Other models have focused on product differentiation, and still others on heterogeneity among firms. These newer models have done a better job of matching the actual patterns of international trade. But the Heckscher–Ohlin model gets to the core trade-off between comparative advantage and power. So it's the right place to start, not least due to its *parsimony*. That is, the model helps us understand when a country should be in a strategic industry in which it's not the most competitive, and when it should trade with other countries that have a comparative advantage.

THE HOLD-UP PROBLEM

A completely different tradition in economics starts not with the nation-state but with an individual transaction as the unit of analysis – a single exchange between a buyer and a seller.

Contracts are almost never complete; it's practically impossible to conceive of all the contingencies that might arise in the future. And even if the contracting parties could conceive of all the contingencies, it is very hard for them to communicate their joint knowledge to an adjudicating court if there's a dispute.

If that sounds a little esoteric, a famous US contract law case from 1960 – taught to every first-year student in American law schools – illustrates just how hard it is for courts to know what the contracting parties really mean.

In *Frigaliment Importing Co. v. B.N.S. International Sales Corp.*, a Swiss buyer contracted with a US seller to purchase "chicken". When the shipment arrived, the buyer found that most of it consisted of older, stewing chickens, rather than young, broiling/frying chickens. This led to a dispute. The buyer claimed that "chicken" meant only young broilers/fryers suitable for grilling. The seller claimed that "chicken" meant any kind of chicken, including older stewing birds. The text of the contract simply specified a "Grade A, Government-inspected chicken".

Ultimately, Judge Henry J. Friendly held that the buyer had failed to prove that "chicken" meant only young chickens. And if a court can't figure out what "chicken" means, what hope do contracting parties have when they enter into more complicated arrangements?

In the mid-1980s, two economists, Sanford Grossman and Oliver Hart, armed with the basic insight that contracts are typically incomplete, asked what the implications of this are for how economic activity is organised. Why do some transactions take place within firms and others in markets?

Contracts cannot specify all future circumstances. So if a contingency not covered by the contract arises, the parties need to renegotiate the terms of their contract. They do so to maximise the value of their relationship. But such a bargain will inevitably split the gains of the renegotiation between the two parties in some way. Anticipating that neither side will receive all the gains from renegotiation, both parties will underinvest in the relationship. They might not tailor their products, plant or equipment as they would have if they stood to receive all the benefits. This is known as the "hold-up problem".

What to do? Well, it might make sense for one party to buy the other party. Then they just negotiate, and split the gains, with themselves. This leads to more investment and more economic surplus.

Grossman and Hart's theory – which has become known as "property rights theory" – implies that the party whose relationship-specific investment is more important should own the other.

In the 2020s, the hold-up problem has gone global ... The unit of analysis is now the nation-state

Consider a coal-fired power station that generates electricity. It wants to locate close to a coalmine to reduce transport costs. There are plenty of coalmines, so the power station can shop around for a good deal on price. But once the power station has chosen a mine and located near it, the market for coal goes from being very competitive to a kind of bilateral monopoly. This doesn't matter if the power station has written a complete contract with the coalmine. A truly complete contract would need to specify things such as the exact quality and grade of coal, when it will be delivered, at what price, in what way, what happens if the delivery is not made, and much more.

To get the most out of the relationship – to maximise the gains from trade – both the power station and the coalmine need to make "relationship-specific investments". For instance, the power station might tailor its plant and equipment to the grade and type of coal it will get from the coalmine. It might build specific receiving docks, for example. Similarly, the mine might invest in specialised equipment to deliver its coal, or to mine ore in a more efficient way. If those investments are also hard to cover in a contract – again, because they're hard to verify to a court – then the cost of them must be borne by each party alone.

In this world of incomplete contracts, therefore, neither party will make the optimal amount of investment. The reason for this is simple. Each party bears all the cost of making its own investment but will get only part of the benefit, because the coalmine and the power station have to haggle as they renegotiate the terms of their contract.

In the case of our power station and coalmine, property rights theory teaches us that whichever party's investment is relatively more important should own the other. If the power station stands to gain more from investing in reducing its costs and enhancing its efficiency, then it should own the coalmine. That way, it doesn't matter so much that it can't write a complete contract. It won't get the efficiencies from the coalmine's investments, but at least it will get *all* the benefits of its own investments. And because it reaps all the benefits (and pays all the costs), it will invest at the most efficient level.

The economic pie is not as big as it would have been if frictionless, complete contracting were possible. But it's bigger than it would have been without vertical integration.

HECKSCHER–OHLIN MEETS GROSSMAN–HART

For four decades, the logic of the hold-up problem has taught economists and practitioners alike about the boundary of the firm.
But here's the thing. In the 2020s, the hold-up problem has gone global. The unit of analysis is no longer just a transaction or even a business. The unit of analysis is now the *nation-state*. It's no longer firms figuring out whether to own their distribution networks or buy their suppliers. It's countries trying to figure out whether to "be in" this industry or that. This is what Trump and Xi, separately and together, have wrought.

This is a whole new problem. And, as outlined above, the way to adapt Grossman and Hart's theory of power inside a firm to the nation-state's use of power is to consider leverage.

Recall that leverage comes in two forms: offensive and defensive. Trump provides obviously the biggest and best example of the offensive use of tariffs. The United States has this power because of the size of its market. That's true for China as well. Plenty of people have wondered what would happen if China simply put a ban on students coming to Australia to study. That would certainly be incredibly painful for Australia but it would also be painful economically for

China. Similarly, it's not in China's economic interest to ban imports of Australian iron ore or coal. And if it's not in their interest, they're unlikely to do it. There's also a political dimension, to which we will return later.

Then there's the defensive leverage of having bargaining chips. Typically, this is going to be more relevant for smaller countries such as Australia, as a way of fending off the United States' and China's use of offensive leverage. Strategic minerals are a bargaining chip. The Pine Gap joint intelligence base in Central Australia is a bargaining chip. And it's plausible that the existence of those two bargaining chips is why the Americans are using less tariff power against Australia than they've wielded against other countries.

An important question is whether defensive leverage is exogenous or can be invested in. In some cases, it's clearly the former. Pine Gap exists and Australia has a large endowment of critical minerals. But in other cases, defensive leverage can be invested in. AUKUS might be an example of this. Australia could also invest in becoming a kind of "critical minerals superpower" by figuring out how to extract them more cheaply, and perhaps even by figuring out how to process them. None of this is likely to be easy or cheap. But there are benefits to it. And often the discussion is based on narrow terms, ignoring the broader economic benefits of building defensive leverage through gaining bargaining chips.

The Trump–Xi era does involve the use of state power but it doesn't entirely eschew comparative advantage. Far from it. So a theory of trade in the Trump–Xi era should involve a combination of power and comparative advantage. The best model of economic power is Grossman–Hart. And the best model of comparative advantage is Heckscher–Ohlin.

The basic economic forces at work in this setting concern the interaction between leverage and factors of production owned in abundance. First, notice that a country either has offensive leverage or does not. It is not industry-dependent, and it is not dependent on other countries. Defensive leverage is also not industry-dependent,

The Trump–Xi era does involve the use of state power but it doesn't entirely eschew comparative advantage

but it is dependent on the pairing of countries. For example, Pine Gap gives Australia defensive leverage only vis-à-vis the United States. Factor abundance, by contrast, is industry-dependent for a given country. If a country has cheap labour, then it will be competitive at textile manufacturing, for example.

Now, suppose Country A (say, the United States) has offensive power but Country B (say, Australia) does not. In an industry where Country B has factor abundance and is therefore an exporter, they will face the prospect of tariffs from Country A. An important question for Country B is whether its factor-abundant industry is a large one or a small one. Or, more precisely, whether the export volumes from Country B to Country A are large or small. If they are large, then defensive leverage will be valuable for this industry. If Country B has many such large industries, then defensive leverage will be particularly important. This would justify further investment in creating defensive leverage.

Another important case to consider is where both countries have offensive leverage – as in the United States–China setting. What happens in a particular industry depends on whether one country is factor-abundant and the other scarce. In that case, the scarce country shouldn't be concerned about the trade patterns and shouldn't impose tariffs, because doing so will only hurt its own domestic consumers.

Of course, one might think that this is a pretty bad depiction of what President Trump has done with tariffs. If one thinks – as I do – that he's using tariffs as a very inefficient revenue-raising exercise, then he is just taxing most imports a lot. That said, Trump has provided exemptions for a number of product categories that he considers strategic (such as semiconductors) or that are major inputs for US producers (such as lumber, critical minerals and energy products).

I'm under no illusion that this is a complete analysis. And none of it is formal. But it perhaps provides some of the ingredients that might be used in a more complete and more formal analysis.

THE POLITICS OF IT ALL

That was the economics of it all – or at least a version of the economics. But it would be naive and dangerous to think that the economics and the politics of our current moment are separable. There has been a significant backlash against neoliberalism. Not only has the actual neoliberalism of Thatcher and Reagan fallen out of vogue, so has the perceived or alleged neoliberalism of Hawke–Keating, Clinton and Blair.

It's striking that the governments of those four leaders are now routinely referred to as being neoliberal. Centre-left governments that believed in a strong welfare state and in providing dignity for all citizens are described by the same insult as the folks who said "there's no such thing as society" and "government isn't the solution to our problems, government is the problem".

Any government that puts too much weight on comparative advantage runs the risk of being branded as neoliberal and losing significant electoral support on the left. In Australia, that might manifest as the Labor Party losing seats to the Greens, or the Liberal Party losing seats to Labor.

On top of this, the use of state power is inherently interventionist, which opens the door to the use of it for political advantage. Labor's recent bailouts of smelters in politically important states and constituencies were surely motivated by that consideration, at least in part.

This suggests that political considerations push the balance between power and comparative advantage away from where the pure economic trade-off would have it. In particular, because political considerations make the use of power more attractive and the use of comparative advantage less attractive, they lead to a greater use of power and a lesser use of comparative advantage. That is, by definition, bad for economic growth. It shrinks the pie.

Trump and Xi, for separate ideological reasons, have changed the global economic landscape. I've referred to it as a "new era". It's worth pausing to reflect on how persistent this era will be. It's likely that Trump will not be president on 20 January 2029. At some point, Xi will no longer be the leader of China. A useful thought experiment is to consider what would happen if Trump and Xi were no longer the leaders of their countries. Would the use of state power recede, meaning a return to the era of globalisation? Would Australia exit critical minerals? Or stop investing in them?

The cheap answer is that it depends on who their successors are. A more complete answer would analyse the forces that led to their rise as leaders, their use of power and whether they are unique figures in the political history of their respective countries. Is there "Trumpism" without Trump? And is there "Xi Jinping Thought" without Xi?

Those are questions best left to others. ■

THE FIX

SOLVING AUSTRALIA'S FOREIGN AFFAIRS CHALLENGES

Robert Law on how Australia can promote trade, investment and tech collaboration with Indonesia

"Australia should build on its success in establishing international campuses in Indonesia and form a government–university partnership that will foster the next generation of Indonesian startups."

THE PROBLEM: Australia's security relationship with Indonesia is in rude health. President Prabowo Subianto and Prime Minister Anthony Albanese announced the landmark Australia–Indonesia Treaty on Common Security in November 2025, hot on the heels of the 2024 Defence Cooperation Agreement. Prabowo's flying visit to Sydney to announce the new treaty had something in common with Albanese's May 2025 visit to Indonesia: neither was accompanied by a business delegation or substantive commercial deals.

The Australia–Indonesia relationship is akin to a three-legged stool, resting on security, economic and people-to-people links. While the security leg is strong, the others are wobbly. If the relationship is to survive the inevitable tests that will come its way in this tumultuous geopolitical world, then the other legs need strengthening.

Despite significant efforts by Canberra to nudge Australian businesses towards Indonesia, progress is slow. Indonesia is Australia's tenth-largest goods export partner. Australia was ranked as the eighth-largest foreign investor in Indonesia in 2024, an improvement on previous years but still only comprising around US$1 billion in value.

For Australia, Indonesia, despite its size, does not offer the same scale and profit margins as more established markets such as China. On the investment side, Australia lacks the industrial base that allows countries such as Japan and Korea to capture political interest by regularly announcing multi-billion-dollar investments.

Economic complementarity between our two countries has limits. Indonesia competes with Australia as an exporter of natural resources such as liquefied natural gas, coal and nickel. And despite a shared interest in establishing an integrated elective vehicle supply chain, no deals have been announced. Yet there are promising sectors: agriculture, food and beverage industries perform strongly, and the digital economy and health sector offer growing opportunities.

Perhaps the most notable success story in recent years is education. Under legislation introduced in 2021, Australia has led the way as the first country to establish international university campuses in Indonesia: Monash University in Greater Jakarta, Western Sydney University in Surabaya, and Deakin University in Bandung (in partnership with Lancaster University and Navitas). Australia should look for opportunities to double down on this area of success, where we have a comparative advantage.

THE PROPOSAL: Australia should build on its success in establishing international campuses in Indonesia and form a government–university partnership that will foster the next generation of Indonesian startups. The partnership would operate across all three university campuses, identifying and nurturing startups and providing the best with seed capital.

There is a particular need for this program in Indonesia, which is reeling from a crisis in its tech sector. Several high-profile startups have been rocked by allegations of corruption and financial malpractice. eFishery, one of Indonesia's "unicorns", reached a valuation of US$1.4 billion in 2023 and attracted investment from Singapore's Temasek and Japan's Softbank. But the company collapsed after the founder admitted to cooking the books, despite regular audits and extensive due diligence by sophisticated investors. This was followed by allegations of corruption and money laundering at TaniHub, including manipulation of financial reports to secure investment from prominent venture capital firms owned by state-owned enterprises.

These cases have made Indonesia's startup sector less attractive to investors, which is stymying business innovation and growth. Venture capital funding dropped to just US$78 million in the first half of 2025, down from US$200 million in the previous six months.

Australian universities are well-placed to help address this crisis through their campuses in Indonesia. The startup program would need to attract talented founders from across Indonesia and not be limited to students at those campuses. Partnerships with Indonesian universities and businesses would be essential to generate interest in the program. Founders and their teams would work with experienced startup coaches and mentors to develop their offerings. Finding the right staff will be crucial. The program needs to be run by experienced innovation practitioners from both countries, not development advisers.

As startups grow, they can recruit new graduates from the international campuses or Indonesian students who have studied in Australia. The training that many of the new employees will need can be provided via short courses and other study options delivered by the campuses. Startups that progress to raising capital could look to Australian university-linked venture and commercialisation funds.

A phased roll-out will be crucial. Classes at the Western Sydney University campus only started in 2024 and at the Deakin University campus in 2025. These universities will need time to bed down their operations and grow their student cohorts. The initiative could start at Monash University, which was established in 2021, and expand to the other campuses over time.

Importantly, the partnership would need investment from the Australian government and the universities, to fund operations and provide capital to invest in promising startups. This will be essential so that all parties have skin in the game. If universities are merely service-delivery partners for government, they will be less inclined to give their full support. The funding commitment should be a minimum of seven years, and ideally ten. This is the timeframe with which venture capital investors work to see a return on their investment.

WHY IT WILL WORK: This initiative aligns squarely with the priorities of the new Indonesian administration. While former president Joko Widodo wanted to be known for building infrastructure, President Prabowo champions social assistance and developing the workforce. Anchoring the initiative in Australian university campuses aligns with this and gives a first-mover advantage as no other country has independently established campuses.

Indonesia aspires to reach high-income status by 2045. McKinsey estimates the country will need to boost its productivity by 1.6 times and drastically increase its number of medium and large companies. Achieving this goal will depend on the creation of successful startups.

Indonesia already has dozens of accelerator programs and venture capital funds, of variable quality. Some are linked to conglomerates that have a vested interest in buying out new technologies developed by startups, rather than letting them grow.

Australian universities have extensive experience in ventures and innovation. For instance, the Melbourne Accelerator Program at the University of Melbourne has operated for over ten years and trained more than 100 founders. Western Sydney University has its own Launch Pad startup incubator, which it has committed to expand to Indonesia. Many Australian universities have launched innovation and commercialisation funds in recent years.

This initiative deepens education ties at the same time as the Australian government's informal cap on international students limits the number of Indonesians who can study in Australia. Economic pressures facing middle-class Indonesians will make study at international campuses in Indonesia an increasingly affordable alternative to studying abroad. The initiative will also help to rebuild investor confidence in Indonesia's startups. It will inject Australian perspectives around business governance, due diligence and financial management.

Australian universities can play a role in nurturing the next Indonesian tech champions that will create jobs and drive innovation, helping to strengthen the economic and people-to-people links that underpin the Australia–Indonesia relationship.

Robert Law is a board member of the Australia-Indonesia Institute. The views expressed do not reflect those of the Australian government.

Review: Luke Brown

INDONESIA

Bomb Season in Jakarta: A Personal Account of a Turbulent Period in Australian Diplomacy
Grant Dooley
Affirm Press

One of the first phrases you learn in the Department of Foreign Affairs and Trade's Indonesian-language program is "*Hubungan Australia–Indonesia mengalami pasang surut*" – that our diplomatic relationship experiences ups and downs. This phrase appearing so early in the language and history curriculum for diplomats and other government staff being sent to Indonesia speaks not just to the roller-coaster of diplomatic dramas that are certain to follow but also to the fact that the Indonesian word for "understatement" is a tongue twister for more advanced learners.

Everyone posted to Jakarta comes home with their share of bureaucratic war stories and diplomatic misunderstandings. But the years covered in Grant Dooley's raw memoir of his Indonesia posting, *Bomb Season in Jakarta*, were something else entirely. Dooley worked in the country from 2004 to 2007 and witnessed the bombing of the Australian embassy in Jakarta, the aftermath of the Boxing Day tsunami in Aceh, the second Bali bombing and the crash of Garuda flight 200 in Yogyakarta.

This book is not a nuanced historical or political analysis of the era in which global terror came for Australians on our own doorstep. Rather, it is a deeply personal narrative. Panic attacks in recent years led Dooley to journal his experiences as a form of therapy, and he sat alone after long days in his finance career, writing out, over Heinekens in a Singaporean pub, the stories he couldn't talk through in therapy. Dooley's unvarnished first-person style makes for compelling reading; this book is utterly unlike the more cerebral tomes in the canon of Australian diplomatic non-fiction.

Most diplomatic memoirs are the reflections of elder statesmen who have lived lives in diplomacy. These volumes tend to be the end-of-career recollections of senior leaders, less about the day-to-day work of junior officers than about how careful interventions with presidents and prime ministers swung global events, and about how steel-cut oats can support metabolism in older age. And yes, until Sue Boyd's excellent memoir *Not Always Diplomatic*, their authors were all men – perhaps unsurprising for a department that, until recently, had more meeting rooms named for flowers than for the many extraordinary women who had served it.

Dooley's book straddles two extremes, covering the minutiae of life on a DFAT posting, interspersed with the drama of the events he witnessed. It will appeal to anyone interested in Australia's foreign dealings or in learning more about how an embassy works, or who enjoys a well-written real-life thriller. But there is a specific value here for those interested in a diplomatic career representing Australia abroad.

When I joined DFAT in 2011, the best advice on training for the job was to study episodes of *Yes Minister* and *The Hollowmen*. There remains no better guide to understanding how policy really gets made, and how "frank and fearless" advice can influence that process. But *Bomb Season in Jakarta* makes a unique contribution by showing readers the real work of a diplomat overseas.

The book has important lessons on the importance of building your own community away from home, and on the unique aesthetic of the department's residential furniture allocations. There are lessons on how careers in the department work too, through Dooley's path and that of several now senior diplomats.

Dooley describes the way in which ministerial requests displace all other diplomatic and personal priorities. He recollects scampering across town after the bombing of his office that morning, still covered in soot and blood, to find suitable luxury accommodation for then foreign minister, Alexander Downer. For diplomats this resonates deeply: everything stops for a ministerial visit. I've seen weddings moved, colleagues recalled from important negotiations and senior officials spending hours resolving scheduling conflicts and seating charts to suit the whims of the travelling minister.

Dooley also recounts the frustration he felt at Downer's staff complaining, just the day after the embassy bombing, that the minister's Scotch was not in his room. Such stories are lore in the department. Kevin Rudd famously required the pressing of suits between landing and the first meeting, a one-hour window – a trivial thing to arrange in London but diabolical in Port Moresby. Julie Bishop required a security-cleared runner capable of a six-minute kilometre to meet her at 5 a.m. to run five kilometres. Again, easier to achieve in Central Park than in central Dhaka.

Throughout the book there are stories of resourcefulness and resilience among Australian diplomatic staff working in difficult circumstances abroad. Despite his horror at seeing colleagues perishing in the burning fuselage of Garuda flight 200, Dooley is quickly at work establishing a coordination point, mobilising staff to check local hospitals and feeding information to Canberra as it arrives on possible consular priorities. The lesson here is that when Canberra wants something to happen, it gets done. But almost anything Canberra wants to do abroad has an Australian diplomat assigned to it, and often they're working in difficult circumstances with limited resources to get an outcome that is in all our interests.

This is the greatest value of this book: it conveys the purpose of the network of public servants that Australia keeps abroad. Our foreign service has long lacked the cachet of its counterparts in the United States,

Europe or parts of Asia. Perhaps that is one legacy of a department that didn't fully poke its head out from behind the imperial apron until the 1970s. And despite having the nation's best negotiators and advocates abroad, the department has long struggled to articulate its value at home. This might explain why successive governments have cut the departmental budget over decades without electoral consequences.

"Doing more with less" has long been the departmental mantra. But part of the resourceful picture Dooley paints, in my experience, reflects a darker truth: that there is never enough money and never enough people. Diplomacy is a career that remains a vocation, in a world of gig work. And it's one that hasn't fully adapted to a world of two-income households, where staff can no longer assume that their partner will up stumps and move around the world on a whim. This dissonance presents a serious threat to staff retention, and therefore to the efficacy of our human capital abroad.

In welcoming this book, politicians current and former have lauded the role of Australia's diplomats and called for greater recognition of their service. The fact is that opportunities to represent Australia abroad, for those of us without the skills to secure a baggy green, really don't get any better than the red passport, and the vast majority of diplomats alongside whom I've worked understand the privilege and work their guts out. But that deep sense of service and obligation needs an adequate investment in the resources our diplomats require, not only for our foreign policy to be as effective as our global circumstances demand but also to make sure we don't stretch people too far.

Dooley's most important lesson for the aspiring and serving diplomat is to look after yourself. His therapy resulted in recovery and this excellent book. But far too many overworked and overstretched Australian diplomats are carrying their own traumas from service in hostile environments abroad, leaving a trail of broken relationships and poor health. We owe them better.

Review: Anthony Milner

SOUTH-EAST ASIA

From Southeast Asia to Indo-Pacific: Culture, Identity, and the Return to Geopolitics
Amitav Acharya
Penguin Random House

This book comes at the right time for Australia. We have begun to focus on South-East Asia again, having been obsessed in recent years with the growing United States–China contest. The problem is that much Australian commentary on this region – and on the Association of Southeast Asian Nations (ASEAN) – is ill-informed. Acharya, a world leader in the study of international relations, takes ASEAN seriously, and this book should stimulate intelligent debate.

South-East Asia – the region of Asia closest to Australia – probably received more attention here during the turbulent post–World War II years, when countries there were emerging from colonial rule. We were an advanced country, willing to provide development aid and advice – but those days are gone.

Today, the South-East Asian countries are together our second-largest trading partner, well ahead of the United States. They have a combined gross domestic product comparable to that of India and Japan, and they have passed the European Union to be China's largest trading partner. ASEAN institutions (including the East Asia Summit, the ASEAN Regional Forum, the ASEAN Defence Ministers' Meeting Plus and the Regional Comprehensive Economic Partnership) offer Australia the opportunity to dialogue with, and potentially work with, all the major states of Asia.

Acharya is optimistic about South-East Asia, though he highlights the challenges ahead. The region is enormously complex, influenced by Islam in some areas, and by Buddhism, Confucianism and Christianity in others. During the colonial period, the region was further divided – among four European empires and the United States. In the twentieth century, Japanese and Indian intellectuals sought to promote a wide "Asian" unity, an anti-colonial regionalism that began to gain influence in South-East Asia. After the Pacific War, Burmese leader Aung San spoke of the need to "rediscover our Asian destiny" and anticipated the forming of a "Southeast Asia" entity and then a "bigger union" with "other parts of Asia".

This is exactly what happened. ASEAN was launched in 1967 by just five states (Indonesia, Malaysia, the Philippines, Singapore and Thailand). Not only were all the countries of South-East Asia then brought into the association, but a wider community was forged with China, Japan and South Korea in the ASEAN Plus Three cooperation process. The 1962 China–India War gave the South-East Asians the opportunity for leadership – and Acharya, in this book and earlier work, has done more than anyone to explain how the ASEAN elite fostered a sense of South-East Asian identity and established institutions and norms to underpin the wider "East Asia" unity.

Acharya notes the criticism that ASEAN is "toothless and clueless" – a view often encountered in Australian commentary – and admits there has been "squabbling" among its members, including over China relations. He also notes challenges faced in advancing human rights and democracy, but suggests the current wave of populism threatens democratic more than authoritarian-leaning states. South-East Asian "strongmen" do not face the same electoral needs to compromise with populist programs.

It is Acharya's positive take on ASEAN that is likely to interest, or provoke, Australian readers. The fault lines within ASEAN, he suggests, should not be exaggerated; nor has its defence spending increased as a share of GDP, or indicated "outright intra-ASEAN competition". Gaining popular commitment to South-East Asian regional unity has not been easy, but surveys show a growing tendency for people to see themselves as "ASEAN citizens".

Beyond South-East Asia, ASEAN has become "the main anchor of regional cooperation involving all the major powers of Asia and indeed the world". True, the international circumstances in which ASEAN operates are more favourable than those in Europe a century ago that led to war with a rising Germany. Acharya takes a relatively sanguine view of major-power rivalry – noting, for instance, that China is not threatening the "metropolitan territory" of any ASEAN state. Economic entanglement is critical. Much trade is now intra-Asian – and, especially with growing inter-state production networks, this "increases the cost of war". Furthermore, ASEAN today is not facing a "multipolar" world – one dominated by great powers – but a "multiplex" world in which smaller states, international institutions and all manner of non-governmental organisations and corporations have agency.

For this new context, ASEAN is well prepared – more so than "minilateral" institutions such as the Quad, in which the United States comes together with Australia, India and Japan, isolating China. True, ASEAN unity is vital and must be maintained. But ASEAN has the advantage of a fundamentally inclusive strategic culture. Its institutions possess impressive "convening power with normative and social leadership", bringing together not only the large North-East Asian states but also the United States and Russia. None of the larger powers could replace ASEAN, because of "mutual distrust and a lack of legitimacy". In this sense, "great power competition does not undermine but supports ASEAN's centrality". Acharya asks: "[W]hat might be Asia's security order today had there been no ASEAN?"

As they watch ASEAN in 2026 deal with the Myanmar and Thai–Cambodian crises and seek warm relations with all the major powers, Australians and others need to know more about the principles guiding South-East Asian foreign relations. Acharya has thought hard about what has been called the "ASEAN Way" and his book provokes further reflection, including about its historical origins.

One principle obvious in ASEAN's handling of the United States, China and Russia is its determination to be "friends to all". Analysts often describe this as "hedging" but Acharya wisely prefers the term "co-engagement". For many years, Malaysian leaders have emphasised the need for a "principled" foreign policy, and there is plenty of evidence that the "friends to all" approach goes back many centuries. The stress on "non-interference" in a foreign state's domestic affairs, which causes frustration for those (including Acharya) who want ASEAN to intervene more decisively in Myanmar, also has deep origins – deeper than the concept of "sovereignty", which is not mentioned in ASEAN's founding document. Like the persistent stress on "consensus", however, non-interference can be seen to underpin ASEAN's "inclusivity" – its patient handling of differences between member states and its willingness to engage other nations, regardless of their internal political arrangements. Analysts often say that non-interference and consensus damage ASEAN, but both might be viewed as supporting, not hindering, ASEAN unity, and "ASEAN centrality" in the wider Asian region.

Acharya might have said more about the strategic heritage of South-East Asia. A book he wrote recently with Manjeet S. Pardesi, *Divergent Worlds*, warns that much modern international relations analysis is shaped by the European heritage of the ancient Mediterranean, and suggests that the international order of the Indian Ocean provides an alternative, less violent history. *From Southeast Asia to Indo-Pacific* takes up the question of the "lenses" through which we "describe 21st century realities in Asia", but it could have delved further.

Discussing academic writing on South-East Asian history, Acharya notes the tradition of "autonomous history" – which focuses on local narratives (local perspectives, experience and agency) when examining the expansion of Indian, Islamic and Western influence across South-East Asia. This type of analysis, which has been influential in Australia, can help explain the origins – and the tenacity – of key operating principles in ASEAN's strategic culture. Apart from showing how firmly embedded dictums such as "friendly to all" and "non-intervention" are, it can throw light on South-East Asia's generally relaxed approach to hierarchical relations: often engagement with superior powers is seen as something to be leveraged rather than feared.

The matter of lenses is especially relevant for Australian commentators. Situated where we are in the world, Australians would do well to study the traditions of foreign relations in our region – and not to interpret the behaviour of our increasingly significant neighbours merely in terms derived from Europe.

CORRESPONDENCE

"The challenge: Reviving nuclear arms control diplomacy"

by Gareth Evans

Melissa Parke

Gareth Evans ("The Challenge", Australian Foreign Affairs 25) makes a compelling case – on moral, legal and rational grounds – for reviving nuclear arms control and disarmament diplomacy. With several thousand nuclear weapons still poised for use around the world, not to mention the increased risk from the integration of AI into military systems, we remain at all times just a hair's breadth from catastrophe. Yet very little is being done to address this grave and growing threat to humanity and our planet.

Eighty years after the US atomic bombings of Hiroshima and Nagasaki – atrocities that claimed more than a quarter of a million lives and left scars across generations – we must work with renewed urgency and determination to bring the era of nuclear weapons to a permanent end. Achieving this goal is in every nation's interests. I hope Evans' stark warning serves as a wake-up call to decision-makers in Australia and beyond.

Although they are legally obligated to pursue negotiations for nuclear disarmament, the nuclear-armed states continue to squander more than US$100 billion every year "modernising" and expanding their arsenals. None is engaged in any serious efforts to advance a nuclear-weapon-free world, and most no longer even pay lip service to the idea. It's a dire state of affairs – although I'm less pessimistic than Evans is about the prospects for charting a new course.

I see great merit in the landmark Treaty on the Prohibition of Nuclear Weapons (TPNW) as a path forward. It was adopted at the United Nations in 2017 and has been in force since 2021;

more than half of all nations have joined it, with more expected to do so in coming years. The treaty fills a major gap in international law, placing nuclear weapons on the same legal footing as other weapons of mass destruction.

Evans accepts the treaty's value as a tool for stigmatising and delegitimising nuclear weapons, including by drawing greater attention to the catastrophic consequences of their use, but he remains sceptical about its potential impact without the participation of nuclear-armed states.

He considers it unlikely that any of the nuclear-armed states or their allies under "nuclear umbrellas" will ever sign on. These, he says, are "the states that matter". But surely the hundred states that have already joined it matter too? Some have populations ten times greater than Australia's. At the very least, their adherence reinforces non-proliferation norms. But more than that, it sends a clear message to nuclear-armed states that their actions are unacceptable and must change.

It's deeply regrettable that Australia remains outside the treaty, when most of our neighbours have ratified it, including Indonesia, New Zealand, Fiji, Malaysia, the Philippines, Thailand and Vietnam. Under the Coalition government in 2017, Australia opted not to participate in the treaty's negotiation, spuriously claiming that the accord risked undermining the Treaty on the Non-Proliferation of Nuclear Weapons (NPT) of 1968 – an agreement limiting possession of nuclear weapons to a handful of states. Evans rightly dismisses that argument and certain other oft-stated concerns about the TPNW.

For him, and perhaps also for the Australian government, the sticking point is the TPNW's prohibition on any form of assistance with nuclear-weapon-related activities, which would pose challenges for our longstanding alliance with the United States, including with respect to joint facilities – notably Pine Gap. But surely extricating ourselves from US preparations for nuclear warfighting is an important step to take if we're serious about advancing disarmament. It wouldn't mean an end to the alliance but rather its reconfiguration. In our region, the Philippines' ratification of the treaty in 2021 has shown how military cooperation between the United States and a state party can continue unimpeded.

For Australia, joining the TPNW would also require us to dispense with the pretence of protection from the US nuclear umbrella. As Evans notes, our ally "will never contemplate sacrificing Miami for Melbourne". He offers an excellent critique of the theory of nuclear deterrence more generally, based on historical example and logic.

It's my strong sense that most Australians want nothing to do with nuclear weapons and think they ought to be eliminated. Our country has made significant contributions in the past to addressing the nuclear threat, as Evans highlights, and "we can again, even in an environment as dispiriting as the one we now confront". The most obvious starting point for Australia would be to sign the TPNW.

At its national conference in 2018, the Australian Labor Party resolved to do just that when in government, after taking account of the treaty's verification architecture, its interaction with the NPT and the progress made in bringing more countries on board. It was Anthony Albanese who proposed the new policy, based on personal conviction. "I don't argue that this is easy. I don't argue that it's simple. But I do argue that it's just," he said at the time. "Nuclear weapons are the most destructive, inhumane and indiscriminate weapons ever created. Today we have an opportunity to take a step towards their elimination."

Now he must act on that commitment for a more peaceful and secure world.

Melissa Parke is the executive director of the International Campaign to Abolish Nuclear Weapons (ICAN) and a former federal Labor parliamentarian and minister.

Allan Behm

Gareth Evans' challenge to the Albanese government to get back into serious arms control diplomacy (Australian Foreign Affairs 25) is necessary and overdue. While the nuclear weapons states modernise their arsenals and improve their missiles, and proliferators build more bombs, the one treaty that involves nuclear and non-nuclear weapon states mutually – the Treaty on the Non-Proliferation of Nuclear Weapons (NPT) – is sinking into irrelevance.

Evans advocates the moral, legal and intellectual arguments with his trademark energy. To meet the challenge, however, the Albanese government will need to do more than simply restore Australia's dedication to and enthusiasm for the task. It must rediscover the courage and leadership to rebuild the values base on which international agreements ultimately stand and without which they inevitably fall.

Our leaders blithely trumpet that we live in disruptive times. What woeful understatement! We live in destructive times, where dishonesty, fraud, graft, greed and selfishness forge a toxic cocktail that annihilates trust in national institutions and the people who lead them.

In this post-postmodern, post-truth world – the world of News Corp and neoliberalism on steroids – things only need to be said in order to be of equal value to everything else that has been said. "It's all relative" – except of course that very statement, which is about as absolutist as you can get. So nuclear weapons possession is just as valid as non-possession. North Korea and Israel already have nuclear bombs. Countries like Japan, South Korea, Germany and even Australia face growing calls to consider acquiring nuclear weapons. This "everyone's doing it" amorality has atrophied whatever remained of a shared morality across the international community.

The transition into catatonic zombie-ism where everything matters equally and nothing matters at all has dumbed down the existential threat posed by nuclear weapons and normalised their possession and use. President Donald Trump crossed a critical threshold by legitimising tactical nuclear weapon use in conventional warfare in his 2018 Nuclear Posture Review. Russia's President Putin and Foreign Minister Lavrov have taken that to its next logical step by threatening Ukraine with a nuclear strike. So the nuclear weapons states now not only hold each other to ransom – they hold the entire world to ransom. And with Trump taking America back to nuclear weapons testing, in defiance of the Comprehensive Nuclear-Test-Ban Treaty, the world is headed for a nuclear weapons free-for-all.

Once upon a time, Australian governments treated the nuclear threat seriously. Prime ministers like Malcolm Fraser and Bob Hawke, foreign ministers like Andrew Peacock and Gareth Evans, and defence ministers like Kim Beazley considered policy options and pushed an active diplomacy. These days, Australian governments continue to drop the ball. The most recent so-called strategic review and national defence strategy are more preoccupied with how Australia can "punch above its weight" – a recipe for getting flattened – than with how we can secure the wellbeing of the global community and ourselves.

To escape this morass will not be easy. The naysayers, confused, fools and downright malicious seem to have the numbers. They have once again to be persuaded that care and compassion, equity and equality, and honesty and justice work to their advantage as well as that of the entire community.

We can no longer rely on America to do this, if we ever could. We must be self-directed, and we must persuade our friends to do the same. We must act in concert.

Evans is right. To create a safer world, we need to take small steps with determination and energy. Strong advocacy for No First Use (NFU) declarations by all nuclear weapons states, including the nuclear pariahs that must be brought to the table, would be a good start. For Australia, this means leveraging our AUKUS links with America and Britain – currently a one-way street, with Australian cash flowing out and nothing much flowing in – to persuade our two collaborators to adopt strong NFU policies. If this means that America has to walk back President Truman's first (and only) use decision, so be it. It would be a powerful example of leadership.

At the same time, the non-nuclear-weapons states should reinforce the International Atomic Energy Agency's (IAEA) nuclear materials accounting and management system to ensure that there is no diversion to weapons production. At a minimum, this would require all states to apply the highest standard IAEA safeguards to their entire nuclear industries, a step that too many states have been reluctant to take. Enforceable sanctions would be in order.

To achieve this, Australia and our like-minded partners need to reinvest in our diplomacy. More diplomats – better trained, more active, better dispersed and better engaged with civil society – are needed to give substance to the "statecraft" which governments are eager to talk about but slow to transact.

Allan Behm is special adviser for the International & Security Affairs Program at The Australia Institute, Canberra.

Alex Bristow

In "The Challenge" (Australian Foreign Affairs 25), Gareth Evans rightly argues that we cannot give up on efforts to contain the spread and avoid the use of nuclear weapons, even if the prospects for progress on these fronts look dim. Developments since the essay's publication – including reports that the Trump administration may relax uranium enrichment restrictions on South Korea as part of a submarine deal, as well as confused signals about US nuclear testing – demonstrate how rapidly norms are changing. Unfortunately, Evans' prescriptions for mitigating nuclear risks and countering proliferation are liable to be ineffective or counterproductive.

Evans deserves credit for confronting some of the myths and groundless idealism that circulate in the arms-control movement. While he supports the intent of the Treaty on the Prohibition of Nuclear Weapons (TPNW), he justifiably concludes that Australia cannot sign it without terminating its alliance with the United States – which, thankfully, he views as too high a price to pay. He repudiates claims that AUKUS poses a proliferation risk, although he opposes it for other reasons.

Evans' main recommendation is that Australia should campaign for No First Use (NFU). This would involve urging all nuclear-armed states to declare that they would only use nuclear weapons to retaliate against a nuclear attack against themselves or their allies. He scolds Australia for not adequately supporting NFU or its variant, sole purpose (a declaration that the role of nuclear weapons is deterring nuclear threats), when they were considered during the Obama and Biden administrations. But Evans does not explain Canberra's reticence.

Australia has made couched nods in favour of NFU or sole purpose in the past, such as from Stephen Smith when he was foreign minister in 2010. And there remain hints of it in Australia's wafer-thin declaratory policy today. For instance, buried on page 14 of the 2024 National Defence Strategy is a statement that US extended nuclear deterrence and arms control are Australia's best protection against "nuclear escalation".

But Canberra probably baulked at going further to avoid getting ahead of the United States or upsetting Japan, which opposes NFU and sole purpose because it fears conventional overmatch by China. Ministers and officials with memories of the anti-nuclear movement in the 1980s might also have preferred to remain coy rather than stir public debate.

Whatever the cause of Canberra's reserve, it is not in Australia's interest for Washington to rule out the credible threat of nuclear first use. This is because, first, the conventional military balance in the region is tilting in China's favour to such an extent that Australia's remote geography may not shield us. Second, China could plausibly use non-nuclear means, such as cyber attack and sabotage, to inflict damage and societal chaos on a scale potentially comparable to a limited nuclear attack. This threat is not hypothetical: at the 2025 Australian Strategic Policy Institute Defence Conference in June, Rachel Noble, a former director-general of the Australian Signals Directorate, warned that China had planted "cyber dynamite" on our critical infrastructure.

Another reason for Australia to reject NFU is the worrying gap between Beijing's words and its deeds. As ASPI resident senior fellow Rajeswari Pillai Rajagopalan explored in Australian Foreign Affairs 25, China is expanding its arsenal of nuclear-capable missiles designed to hit targets in this region rather than the contiguous United States. These "tactical" weapons are highly accurate and could field nuclear warheads with relatively small explosive yields, suitable for targeting military assets like bases and ships. While Beijing advocates at the United Nations for an NFU treaty, it appears to be reshaping its own arsenal for coercion and fighting limited nuclear wars. North Korea is doing something similar. Both will be avidly studying Russia's nuclear coercion playbook.

To assure allies and deter Beijing, Australia should encourage the United States to deploy more nuclear forces in this region, including shorter-range, low-yield systems that could respond proportionately to China's tactical nuclear arsenal. Australia should, for instance, provide ports and maintenance for US Navy attack submarines, which could carry the submarine-launched cruise missile nuclear (SLCM-N) when it becomes operational in the mid-2030s. This can be done legally by exploiting caveats in the South Pacific Nuclear Free Zone.

Such thinking is anathema to Evans because he rejects the credibility of extended nuclear deterrence and portrays the destruction of cities as the crux of nuclear strategy. Reframing Charles de Gaulle's famous remark to John F. Kennedy, he claims that the United States would never sacrifice Miami for Melbourne. In Evans' view, this "has always been the case"; it is not a foible of Donald Trump. Similarly, he argues that Russia would be undeterred by a nuclear-armed Ukraine because Kyiv couldn't credibly carry out threats to destroy Moscow.

As former ASPI senior analyst Rod Lyon has argued, Evans is part of an Australian school of thought, particularly prominent in the Labor Party, that prefers to work in the familiar conceptual surroundings of "mutually assured destruction", which supposedly supports "stable" deterrence, rather than grapple with a world in which limited nuclear war is possible. Unfortunately, we cannot ignore that our adversaries seem to hold a different view.

I support Evans' call for the Australian prime minister to give a major speech on nuclear issues. But my speaking notes would look different. I would encourage the prime minister to tell the Australian public, in plain terms, why we need to actively strengthen the US nuclear umbrella, including by hosting more visiting nuclear forces. Reinforcing deterrence in this way would do more to avert nuclear war than grandstanding for NFU.

Alex Bristow is a senior analyst at the Australian Strategic Policy Institute.

Gareth Evans responds

Melissa Parke and Allan Behm both get it, but Alex Bristow remains in denial. About the indefensible inhumanity of any nuclear weapons use; about the existential risk that any large-scale nuclear exchange would pose for life on this planet as we know it; about the risk of use flowing as much from human or system error as from deliberative aggression; about the essentially illusory nature of nuclear deterrence in today's world; and about the utility of Australia re-engaging in serious nuclear arms control diplomacy.

In the Parke and, especially, Behm comments, but conspicuously absent in Bristow's, there is a strong moral as well as rational dimension. That must remain the starting, if not finishing, point in this debate. Yes, massive damage can be inflicted by conventional weaponry and, as Bristow insists, by cyber attacks and sabotage. But nuclear weapons remain in a class of their own, the most indiscriminately inhumane ever devised, and the only ones posing an existential risk to our common humanity. They deserve to be regarded with even more of the instinctive horror the world seems to currently reserve for biological and chemical weapons, both effectively now universally banned.

I share Parke's passionate commitment to complete abolition and would be delighted if the Treaty on the Prohibition of Nuclear Weapons (TPNW) could ever become the vehicle for achieving that. The support of its current adherents – more than half the world's states – of course matters, as she insists, and I fervently hope that the treaty continues to expand its base and build normative momentum for change. My point is simply that here, as so often in public policy, the best should not be the enemy of the good. Given both the treaty's structural flaws and the total hostility of all the present nuclear-armed states to ever embracing it, our campaign priorities would be more productively focused on nuclear risk reduction, starting with universal commitment to No First Use (NFU).

For Australia to join the TPNW, as Parke so strongly advocates (and to stop ducking and fudging the issue, as the Albanese government has been doing), would certainly do wonders for our global anti-nuclear credentials. But the difficulties this would pose for our US alliance really are currently insuperable. Much more than a Philippines-style "reconfiguration" would be involved, given the ever-increasing scale of the commitment we have now made to American nuclear strike capability, with new submarine and B-52 bases in Western Australia and the Northern Territory now joining Pine Gap. I am one of the many Australians whose belief is now much less reflexively strong than it used to be that, in this Trumpian age, the benefits of the alliance outweigh any potential costs. But I can only repeat my conclusion that putting ANZUS at risk "is rather a lot to bite off as the price of joining a treaty with no practical teeth".

Alex Bristow's comment makes three major criticisms, all demanding reply. The first is that I prefer to "work in the familiar conceptual surroundings of 'mutually assured destruction' ... rather than grapple with a world in which limited nuclear war is possible". Nuclear weapons enthusiasts, always keen to make their use more rationally feasible, have long been enchanted with the idea of winnable limited nuclear war, and the viability of "escalating in order to de-escalate". It goes back to Herman Kahn and Albert Wohlstetter in the 1960s and 1970s (whose approach has been characterised aptly as replacing MAD with NUTS: "nuclear utilisation target selection"). And it has in recent years been embraced again in US Nuclear Posture Reviews – and by the Pentagon's legion of Australian acolytes in the Australian Strategic Policy Institute and elsewhere.

The idea is that nuclear warfighting operations using lower-yield "tactical" weapons can be conducted with cool precision and control, with the adversary reading the signal of limited use as intended and responding with appropriate restraint.

But there is an extensive body of literature challenging that assumption and referring to multiple wargames in which supposedly calibrated attacks have almost invariably resulted not in capitulation but in escalation. Add to that the implications, for "limited-damage" enthusiasts, of the reality that modern "tactical" nuclear warheads have yields up to many times those of the weapons used in Hiroshima and Nagasaki. And, even more alarmingly, the implications, including for non-proliferation, of breaching the longstanding taboo against any use of nuclear weapons, challenged recently by Russia but still critical for nuclear risk reduction.

The second issue that divides us is the notion that China's military build-up, "reshaping its own arsenal for coercion", demands nothing less than nuclear deterrence from the United States and its allies and partners. As with so many of his like-minded colleagues in the defence and intelligence, think-tank and conservative media community, Bristow over-eggs the China-threat pudding. There is certainly much in China's behaviour to warrant regional security concern. But most of it is no more than can and should be expected of a hugely trade-dependent economic superpower, resentful of any continuing claim by America to unchallenged primacy in regional and global affairs, and wanting to claim its own strategic space, and to generally reassert some of its historical greatness after more than a century of wounded national pride.

There is no reason to assume that China would ever contemplate outright military aggression – Hitler, Tojo or Putin style – against any of its sovereign neighbours, let alone the United States. Taiwan remains a special case, a flourishing democracy and distressingly vulnerable, but recognised by no one as a Kuwait or Ukraine style sovereign entity. Military preparedness of course has to be based on potential adversaries' capability, not their presumed intent, but for the foreseeable future America's immense conventional firepower, combined with that of its potentially affected allies and partners, should be amply sufficient to deter any conceivable kinetic threat.

Bristow's third criticism is that my risk-reduction agenda, with NFU its centrepiece, is "liable to be ineffective or counterproductive", and that "it is not in Australia's interest for Washington to rule out the credible threat of nuclear first use". But I remain wholly convinced that retaining a first-use option is dangerous, both for wider global peace and security and often for nuclear-armed states' own interests, and that advancing NFU should be Australia's highest arms control priority.

A nuclear-armed state that keeps a first-strike option runs the risk of an adversary misreading its intentions and, fearing decapitation, launching a pre-emptive strike, precipitating an otherwise wholly avoidable nuclear war. Again, a nuclear-armed state that fears a surprise first-use attack from another which has kept open that option is more likely to put its forces on extreme launch alert, thereby increasing the risk of human or system error or miscalculation causing a launch that precipitates the very catastrophe it is trying to avert.

Moreover, refusing to adopt NFU encourages nuclear proliferation. Vertically (that is, more weapons for existing nuclear powers), because it incentivises potential adversaries to upgrade their own nuclear forces to deny their opponents a first-use advantage or gain one themselves: thus fostering nuclear arms races, with all the multiplication of risk these necessarily involve. And horizontally (acquisition by new players), because when a state with any kind of conventional capability insists that it needs nuclear weapons to deter or defeat non-nuclear attacks, it necessarily concedes that right to any other country fearing, or claiming to fear, such attack.

The bottom line of my article's argument remains this: for all the psychological comfort nuclear weapons seem to give their possessors and advocates, the risks associated with their possession by anyone – not least the risks associated with system or human error, which Bristow acknowledges not at all – far outweigh any potential rewards. But I acknowledge that the force of that argument is anything but self-evident to a great many people, and I welcome the opportunity *Australian Foreign Affairs* has given me and my three spirited commentators to debate its merits in these pages.

Gareth Evans was Australia's Foreign Minister from 1988 to 1996 and president of the International Crisis Group from 2000 to 2009.

THE BACK PAGE
Foreign policy concepts and jargon, explained

Third nuclear age

WHAT IS IT A view that the world has entered an era of heightened nuclear risk due to the United States–China rivalry, the breakdown of arms controls and the proliferation of tactical nuclear weapons and advanced conventional weapons. Tony Radakin (defence chief, UK) believes the era is defined by "proliferating nuclear and disruptive technologies, and the almost total absence of the security architectures that went before".

WHO COINED IT Michal Smetana (associate professor, Charles University) was among the first to use the term, arguing in 2018 that a third nuclear age had emerged due to the end of the "interregnum" between periods of great-power rivalry.

OTHER AGES The first nuclear age, from 1945 to 1991, was dominated by the Cold War rivalry between the United States and the Soviet Union. In 1996, Fred Iklé (former under secretary of defence, US) wrote that this age had come to "a rather happy ending" and that the main risks in the second age were an increase in nuclear powers and the threat of non-state actors acquiring weapons.

WORST AGE Some scholars believe the third age may be the riskiest. Andrew Futter (professor, University of Leicester) and Benjamin Zala (senior lecturer, Monash University) have warned it involves a dangerous mix of "the major power competition of the First, combined with the more diffuse spread of high-tech weaponry associated with the Second".

ANTI-AGEISM Others disavow nuclear ages. Tom Vaughan (lecturer, Leeds University) has argued that some militaries and strategists trumpet new dangers to justify their arsenals and budgets, describing the third nuclear age as "a conceptual stalking horse for a fresh nuclear arms race".